WHEN A MAN YOU LOVE WAS ABUSED

WHEN A MAN YOU LOVE WAS ABUSED

*A Woman's Guide to Helping Him
Overcome Childhood Sexual Molestation*

CECIL MURPHEY

Kregel
Publications

When a Man You Love Was Abused: A Woman's Guide to Helping Him Overcome Childhood Sexual Molestation

© 2010 by Cecil Murphey

Published by Kregel Publications, a division of Kregel, Inc., P.O. Box 2607, Grand Rapids, MI 49501.

All Scripture quotations, unless otherwise indicated, are from the *Holy Bible*, New Living Translation, copyright © 1996, 2004. Used by permission of Tyndale House Publishers, Inc., Wheaton, Illinois 60189. All rights reserved.

Scripture quotations marked KJV are from the King James Version.

Scripture quotations marked NIV are from the HOLY BIBLE, NEW INTERNATIONAL VERSION®. NIV®. Copyright © 1973, 1978, 1984 by International Bible Society. Used by permission of Zondervan. All rights reserved.

Scripture quotations marked NKJV are from the New King James Version. Copyright © 1982 by Thomas Nelson, Inc. Used by permission. All rights reserved.

The author and publisher are not engaged in rendering medical or psychological services, and this book is not intended as a guide to diagnose or treat medical or psychological problems. If the reader requires medical, psychological, or other expert assistance, please seek the services of your own physician or certified counselor.

Library of Congress Cataloging-in-Publication Data
Murphey, Cecil B.
When a man you love was abused : a woman's guide to helping him overcome childhood sexual molestation / Cecil Murphey.
    p. cm.
1. Male sexual abuse victims—Religious life. 2. Adult child sexual abuse victims—Religious life. 3. Man-woman relationships—Religious aspects—Christianity. I. Title.
BV4596.A25M87   2010   248.8'6—dc22   2009043630

ISBN 978-0-8254-3353-5

Printed in the United States of America

10 11 12 13 14 / 5 4 3 2 1

— Contents —

Part 2. How You Can Help Him

A Word About the Names in This Book

When I write nonfiction books I like to provide the full name of the individuals involved. I believe it adds integrity to the material and shows they're not made-up accounts or composites. In this book, however, I can't do that. This material is much too sensitive and personal.

"If I gave my name," one man said, "my family might find out, and they wouldn't forgive me." His stepfather had been the perpetrator.

Others who talked to me gave no specific reason other than to say, "I'm not ready to tell this publicly" or "I'd rather you don't use my name."

Out of respect for these individuals, I've disguised their identity. If you read only a first name, it's for one of three reasons:

1. The person requested I not use his name.
2. Several of the groups in which I participated are like AA—and we use only our first names. I tell the story of a man named Red, for example, so called because that's the only name by which I knew him.
3. I no longer have contact with the person and couldn't get permission.

How to Use This Book

I've designed this book in two parts, and it doesn't matter which you read first.

Part 1 focuses on male sexual assault and its effects. This part is basically informative, and its purpose is to help you understand the problems that male abuse victims face.

Part 2 is the practical section. The purpose is to show you—a woman in the life of a man who was molested as a child—what you can do to help him.

— *Acknowledgments* —

My deepest thanks

- To the men who, because of their experiences, helped me write this book, and many of whose names I cannot list here: You have been through the horrors of life and survived, and I'm grateful you're able to talk about your pain.

- To Shirley, my wife, and David Morgan, my special friend: You two loved me enough to give me the courage to heal.

- To Deidre Knight, my agent and encourager; and my assistant, Twila Belk, who understood.

- To my editor, Steve Barclift, who believed in this book and courageously took it to his publishing committee.

IF YOU'RE AN IMPORTANT WOMAN IN HIS LIFE

He was molested—or at least you suspect he was. That means he was victimized by someone older and more powerful than he was. The man you care for might be your boyfriend, husband, brother, father, or son. He is someone you care about deeply, and because he hurts, you hurt.

He hurts because he was victimized in childhood. Many therapists don't like the word *victim* or *victimized* and prefer to speak of *survivors*. They also don't like the word *abused* and usually opt for *assaulted*. The media tend to use the word *molested*. In this book, I use the terms interchangeably.

Regardless of the word used, something happened to him—something terrible and frightening—that will affect him for the rest of his life. Something happened to him that affects *your* life as well.

How Can You Help?

Because you care about him, you have also been victimized. Because of your love for him, you've been hurt, and you may have suffered for a long time. But the man you care for didn't hurt you intentionally. He was trying to cope with his problem.

Perhaps years passed before you knew about his childhood pain. During that time, you may have sensed something was wrong. Statistics indicate that men tend to reveal themselves more readily to a woman, usually a wife or girlfriend.

But even if you knew about his experience, how could you have grasped how it would impact your relationship? Because he battled the problem that he couldn't talk about, he did it privately and sometimes not too well. How could you not feel rejected or hurt when he shut you out?

Even if he faced his abuse, he may have excused the perpetrator. Although the man in your life was the victim, he may have felt guilty for the abuse. *His undeserved guilt is real. And he hurts.*

Because he hurts, you hurt too.

That's part of *your* victimization. His reactions, attitudes, and behavior caused you to assume blame and guilt, and you've asked yourself, "How did I fail?" You may not have voiced those words, but you felt you were the flawed person in the relationship.

If this describes you, you may already have gone through a lengthy period of wondering what was wrong with you. You tormented yourself with questions:

+ Why does he shut me out?
+ Why can't I help him?
+ Why can't I take away his pain?
+ Why won't he talk to me or allow me into his private world?
+ How did I fail him?
+ I love him and try to show him that, so why won't he trust me?

If you're reading this, it means you know, or seriously suspect, that an important male in your life was assaulted in childhood. You love him and want to relieve his pain, but you feel helpless. Or you're sure there must be something you can do to fix him. If you could just figure out the hidden weapon, the magic pill, or the right words, he'd be all right.

It isn't that simple. Besides, you can't fix him.

In this book, though, I provide suggestions in part 2 to help you understand and accept him. As you accept his situation and his resulting problems, I hope you'll feel better about yourself and accept that *his problem is not your fault.* You may often need to remind yourself of this fact: it is *his battle.* You can't fight his inner demons, but you can stand with him when he fights them. He must work through it himself. You can assist him by being available to him, and I'll suggest ways to do that. *But it is his struggle and his journey into wholeness.*

You may feel more at peace with your inability to heal him if you can think of him as a once-innocent child who was victimized by a predator. This isn't to deny your pain, but you can help him and help yourself if you can start with understanding something from his past.

His experience and his response to it are complex. He has been wounded in several ways, the old wounds reopen in unpredictable ways, and you can't do anything to make him into a whole person. You can stand with him as he seeks and discovers his own healing. As you accept his situation and his resulting problems and behavior, I hope you'll feel better about yourself and accept the reality that his problem isn't your fault. He must work through his own emotional issues—with your assistance of love and encouragement.

I want to make an important distinction here. When an adult sexually abuses a boy, many people think of that as a sexual act. That's not correct. The perpetrator's actions weren't about sex, and they weren't about love for the child. Those who molest have deep-seated problems that go far deeper than sexual exploitation of a child. For the perpetrator, sexual gratification at the expense of a child is a *symptom* of deeper problems that go beyond the scope of this book.

When adults are attracted to children—compulsively attracted— we call them pedophiles. Although there are variations in the definition of pedophiles, here's a simple one: the term comes from two Greek words—*paidos,* children, and *philia,* a word for love. It refers to anyone—male or female—who is sexually attracted to prepubescent children. I'll say it even stronger; they are *compulsively* attracted. Generally, that means the objects of their desire are children younger than thirteen. Therapists have recorded that some pedophiles visualize themselves as being at the same age as the children they molest. Other therapists would say that pedophiles are adults who are fixated at the prepubescent stage of life.

Just as all assaulted boys won't become homosexuals, the male perpetrator may not be gay. Most of those convicted of molesting boys vehemently deny that they are homosexual and insist they are heterosexual.

Regardless, when an adult molests an innocent child, that's sexual abuse. My intention is not that you try to understand the abuser, or that you feel sorry for that person. By the end of the journey, though, I hope you and the man in your life will be able to forgive and to feel sadness for such individuals.

The perpetrator—whether male or female—is a sexual abuser of children. That's the one fact to bear in mind. Sometimes it makes no difference to the perpetrator whether the victims are male or female. This is an important concept for you, the woman in the victim's life, to understand. The result of his abuse carries long-lasting effects, and he may not want to talk about the issues related to the abuse for fear of being labeled as homosexual. *Or he may feel he is gay because it was a man who molested him.* You may need to help him accept that child sexual abuse is not a heterosexual-homosexual issue. It's a crime and a sin that was perpetrated against him.

He probably doesn't understand all that. He may still feel conflicted about what happened to him—and about the theft of his innocence. For now, the once-abused child needs support and encouragement. He needs someone he can trust as he copes with his pain and his problems. He needs you.

— *Part 1* —

WHO HE IS

— 1 —

WHO ARE THE MOLESTED?

This book came about after I wrote an article for women readers whose husbands had been molested in childhood. More than one hundred copies of *Light and Life* magazine, in which the article appeared, lay on the free sample table at a conference where I taught in California. Many conferees picked up copies.

Although most of them didn't read the article at the conference, several did. Two men told me they appreciated my candor in speaking out. One said, "I think that's a picture of me." His eyes began to tear, and he chose not to talk further.

Three women privately discussed the article with me. "I'm sure my husband was abused," one woman confided. "He won't talk about it, but for years I've believed that he was." When she had asked her husband, he'd say only that he'd experienced such a terrible childhood he didn't want to discuss it. She planned to ask him to read the article and hoped it would be a catalyst for them to talk about his past. She didn't contact me again.

One mother wept as she told me that her older brother had abused her son. The boy admitted it, but the uncle denied the accusation. Whenever she brought up the subject, her eight-year-old son cried and couldn't talk about it. The woman refused to allow her brother to visit and cut off all contact from him. "My son has started counseling," she said, "but so far it hasn't helped."

After the conference, another woman e-mailed me with a similar story. "I talked to my brother, and he admits he was molested," she wrote, "but he won't get professional help. I know he still hurts. His seventh-grade Sunday school teacher was the abuser." Because of the perpetrator, her brother refuses to go to church, "even though he believes in God and reads his Bible."

"I thought I was the only one," one man said when he phoned me and talked for almost half an hour. "I'd heard about girls being molested, but not boys. This is the first time I've ever talked to a man who also went through what I endured." He added, "Intellectually, I know there are thousands of others, but emotionally, my isolation makes me feel as if no one else has been there."

"Yes, I know what it's like to feel as if you're the only one," I said.

✦   ✦   ✦

From responses to my blog, http://shatteringthesilence.wordpress.com, I've learned that many males are afraid to admit they've been abused. It seems related to how they perceive themselves as males. They're often afraid of how others will perceive their manhood.

I understand why they think that way because I experienced similar feelings when I began to cope with my own abusive childhood. In the late 1980s, I became emotionally aware of not being the only one who felt that way. I attended a conference called "Men and Masculinity" that summer at Oglethorpe University in Atlanta. The conference offered seventeen small-group settings. With great hesitancy, I signed up for one called "Men Who Were Sexually Molested in Childhood."

At the time, I'd been in the process for at least a year of healing from my own childhood abuse, but I hadn't spoken with other males who'd been molested. In the small group of seven, each man briefly shared his own heartache over childhood sexual molestation.

I let the others go first. Tears filled my eyes as the first one related his story. His was the first I'd ever heard about a Catholic priest assaulting a boy. One by one the other six told their stories.

When my turn came, I tried to talk, but I couldn't. I couldn't hold back the sobbing. The six men silently formed a circle around me and hugged me.

"We understand your pain," one man whispered.

Fresh sobs came from an even deeper place inside me. My body shook for what seemed like minutes. Until I started to recover from my childhood abuse, I hadn't cried for many years.

"Cry as much as you need to," someone said.

When I finally could talk, I told them my story. For the first time, I felt I had found a safe environment and was able to speak openly about the abuse of my childhood. While I talked, I shifted my gaze from face to face. Each of the six said a kind word, touched my hand or shoulder, or nodded.

That day, all seven of us faced the pain of our childhoods. The others were further ahead in their healing, but we all traveled along the same path. By acknowledging the theft of our innocence, each of us took a few steps toward healing. Three of them were in therapy. Except for me, all of them had talked to at least one professional about being molested.

"It helps to know that I'm not the only one," I said several times, because that was such a powerful revelation for me.

"I used to believe it was my fault," one man in the group said. "I never figured out what I did to make my uncle do those things, so I blamed myself."

"I guess I'd have to say that shame held me back the most," a second man volunteered. "I was sure my friends would laugh at me if I told them what happened. They'd call me gay." He later said that the physical stimulation felt good. "Yet I hated what he did, and I was scared and kept begging him not to do it. For many years afterward, I believed something was wrong with me."

Of the nearly two hundred men who attended the conference, only seven of us attended that small group. *We are seven, but how many others are there?* I wondered. How many more of the conferees had been molested as children? As I learned later, a number of others could have joined us, and they might have gained from the experience.

After the conference one man told me, "I wasn't ready to share with a group, but I need to talk to someone."

We cried together and hugged each other.

✦   ✦   ✦

What percentage of males experience some form of sexual abuse before the age of sixteen? No one knows the answer, and the proposed figure is highly controversial. For many reasons, researchers encounter more resistance in getting that information from males than from females. One of the difficulties the experts face is how to define abuse. Another involves the methodologies used in doing the investigation, such as the way the researchers phrase the questions. There is no clearly agreed-upon method.

Since the 1980s, a large number of organizations have conducted surveys and interviews and ended up with conflicting answers. Critics have often blamed the questionnaire for being either too specific or not clear enough. Others have faulted the lack of honest responses. The number of males abused in childhood are listed as low as 5 percent or as high as 33 percent.

Probably the most accepted figure is one in six boys—but even those who use that figure believe it's conservative. Even if it were one in ten, or one in every thirty, that still means boys are victimized.

One Web site, http://www.1in6.org, states, "Researchers estimate that 1 in 6 males have experienced unwanted or abusive sexual experiences before age 16. This is likely a low estimate, since it doesn't include noncontact experiences, which can also have lasting negative effects."

Emerging evidence indicates as many as a third of incidents of child sexual molestation aren't remembered by adults who experienced them, and that the younger the child was at the time of the molestation, and the closer the relationship to the abuser, the more likely he is not to remember or not to remember clearly.

In recent years, more men are coming forward and admitting that they were assaulted as children by Roman Catholic priests. This development has encouraged others to speak out. And it's not just priests who abuse, and not all priests are guilty. Perpetrators come from all occupations and all faiths.

Despite the revelations of male sexual molestation, our culture still implies that men are supposed to be invulnerable—if a male was molested, something was wrong with the *victim*. That was a common attitude about females a generation ago. Too often, the assaulted male feels he won't be believed. We have that in common with females.

Males also have additional concerns: *Our strongest fear seems either that others will think of us as homosexuals or that something is wrong with us.* Many adult men who have survived sexual abuse as children have questions about their sexual orientation—that is, they question whether they might be gay. "After all," they reason, "I should have resisted the molestation."

Or they might believe they're weak or helpless. "After all, I should have *been able* to resist the molestation." Another fear is that if they go public with their molestation other people will assume that one day the victims will become perpetrators, or that people will scrutinize their activities, fearing the pattern of molestation will repeat itself. Although many men who assault children were themselves victimized in childhood, nothing indicates that most abuse survivors will commit the offense.

Several researchers have posed a theory about which boys are selected for abuse by their perpetrators. Almost all authorities acknowledge that abusers have a special kind of antennae that pick up the frequency of possible victims. I tend to agree.

I've also read, and watched TV programs, about con artists and pickpockets. Those who are successful at their "trade" are intuitive and have an almost-infallible beacon that spotlights the vulnerable. It might be the way potential victims walk or something about the way they dress. Con artists seem to be able to look into a person's eyes and spot the vulnerable and the impressionable.

That's probably just as true with perpetrators and the boys they abuse. One thing I've heard and read several times is that, generally, the victims were characterized by an intense quest for affection. They perceived that one or both parents had rejected them. They were so needy they would have done anything to be loved.

When an adult prepares to molest a boy, then the perpetrator begins by showing interest. Perhaps he's kind and attentive. Because of that attentive kindness the boy is receptive; he needs affection. As the relationship grows, the boy accepts the abuse in silence because he feels loved, accepted, or attached to the other person. He may not like what the older person does to him, but he often is unable to protest or stop the molestation.

A man in his twenties, for example, spoke about being abused by three different men. "I used to wonder if I wore a sign on my forehead that said, 'I've already been abused. Come and use me like they did.'"

Such boys who don't fight back learned that if they are to receive affection, no matter how perverted, they must pay the price with their bodies. Be careful not to blame the boy for being needy. He yearned for affection because he didn't get the kind of attention, acceptance, and love that every child deserves. Because the real thing was denied him—the first and more important victimization—he became vulnerable to the second.

The desire to feel loved is a built-in requirement of every human. Some might not feel loved, so they cry out, "Who needs it? I don't need anybody or anything." That's a powerful act of self-deception. The reality is that every person in the world needs and deserves love. Every person was born to be loved and to be treated lovingly.

Some of those who cry out do so because they don't grasp the meaning of real love. For abused kids, too often the word *love* means sex. It's difficult for them to accept that love is the unselfish giving of themselves and not the giving of their bodies to satisfy the lusts of predators.

Facing the Reality

I hold out hope for, and I encourage women to stand with, the male victims of rape. But I also want you to face reality. Some men won't recover from the trauma of childhood. Even if they are able to talk about their abuse, they may continue to feel the pain every day of their lives. They can't release the anger, or they remain traumatized or refuse to forgive. That's reality—but I hope you'll do whatever you can to help the victims move beyond the pain of their past. Part 2 of this book will help you in doing that.

Every male who has been molested is an individual. What helps one survivor may not help another. Some may experience feelings of pain, fear, anger, and isolation. Some may go the other way and numb out, as I did, and feel nothing.

Despite negative indicators, there is hope. I am a victorious survivor. In this book you'll also read of other men who faced the demons of their childhood, have survived, and now consider themselves healed and healthy.

Because of the grace of God that permeates their horrific childhood, they are able to say,

> All praise to God, the Father of our Lord Jesus Christ. God is our merciful Father and the source of all comfort. He comforts us in all our troubles so that we can comfort others. When they are troubled, we will be able to give them the same comfort God has given us. (2 Corinthians 1:3–4)

They are also the same men who believe,

> We know that God causes everything to work together for the good of those who love God and are called according to his purpose for them. (Romans 8:28)

2

A PERSONAL JOURNEY

I am a male survivor of childhood sexual assault. I want to tell my story so you'll know why this book is important to me.

And it's not just my story. For several years, my wife suffered because neither of us understood the implications of my abuse. I want to tell about my healing, but I also want to point out Shirley's loving support during the recovery. I couldn't have gone through the healing process without her at my side. She supported me even though she didn't at first know about my experience or understand why I behaved as I did.

In some ways I'm one of the lucky male survivors. I "forgot" what happened to me. As I would later realize, that was a form of denial but it became my method of survival. For forty years the pain of abuse lay deeply buried in my subconscious mind. Despite the repression—which is what forgetting is—I grew up living with the *effects* of the molestation even though I no longer remembered my abuse. That is, until a series of emotional disruptions brought them to the surface.

I want to explain that my memories didn't begin to surface through the intervention of a therapist. An area of controversy today called *false memory syndrome* suggests that many who claim childhood abuse have so-called memories inadvertently planted by therapists (see chapter 8). Even though David Morgan, my best friend, is a therapist and has been with me from the beginning of my healing, he carefully avoided any intervention or suggestion of assault. In addition, one of my brothers and two of my sisters later corroborated many of my childhood memories.

Those abusive experiences left their marks on my life. Like thousands of other victims of molestation—male and female—I struggled over many issues. Perhaps the most significant one is that of trust.

It's strange how this issue of trust works. Either we tend to trust no one or we go the other way and trust everyone. I vacillated between the two extremes and rarely lived in the middle. When I felt a connection with anyone—and those connections were usually healthy—I was naive and accepting. No matter what the person told me, I believed it. Worse, I think I idealized the person. For me, that was especially true with older males. Looking back, I'm sure I sought a loving father figure in older men. None of them ever made any kind of sexual advances, but none of them lived up to my expectations either.

Other times I met people who tried to reach out to me, but I pushed them away. I couldn't trust them. I don't know if there was some acute warning bell or if it was part of the result of abuse.

Beyond the issue of trust, there are other issues with which we survivors struggle. Three troubled me most of my adult life:

+ Fear of abandonment
+ A sense of loneliness and aloneness
+ Feeling different from everyone else—and translating the word *different* to mean *bad*

My Story

I became a serious Christian in my early twenties. Months after my conversion, I met Shirley, and we later married. We had five or six problem-free years before a single event changed our marriage.

I had been gone for nearly two weeks. When I came home, Shirley lay in bed, and I thought she was asleep. I climbed in beside her, and in the dark, she turned over and touched me.

I froze.

Feelings of anger and revulsion spread through me. I'd never before had those feelings in our marriage. I didn't understand what was going on inside me. I couldn't respond to her, and I didn't understand the reason. I pushed her arm away and mumbled something about being exhausted.

She rolled over, and although she tried to cover up her tears, I heard the soft sobs. Her pain made me feel worse. *Why had I done such a cruel thing? Why had I pushed her away?*

I lay awake a long time trying to figure it out. *What's wrong with me?* I asked myself repeatedly. No matter how much I prayed, I couldn't understand my angry reaction.

Over the next several years, occasionally I had similar reactions. Looking back, I realize that when she initiated any affection that I hadn't anticipated, especially in the dark, I froze. Each time it happened, I felt guilty and silently begged God to show me what was wrong with me. Slowly my seemingly irrational feelings decreased, and life seemed to resume a loving normalcy.

The next event happened during a long run. I'd been a runner for at least a decade and usually did six or seven miles a day. That morning in the early fall, I decided to do a twelve-mile run, the longest I had ever done. About the tenth mile, sadness came over me—a deep, depressive melancholy. The tears began to flow and I couldn't figure out why. I was sobbing so hard that I had to walk the last half mile.

The painful past had finally broken through. I remembered. The images were vague and unclear, but a memory nonetheless: The old man undressed me and fondled me. I also remembered the female relative who assaulted me.

I didn't want to believe such memories. Some days I convinced myself that I had conjured up terrible thoughts about innocent adults. Most of the time, however, I *knew*. It wasn't my imagination, and it had happened. If that was so, why hadn't I remembered it before? Why now?

After that, crying became almost a daily routine. I usually ran for about an hour very early in the mornings. On many of those runs, tears would stream down my face before I finished. A few mornings I sat on the curb in the dark and cried until I was able to get up and run again.

Over the next few weeks, other childhood memories crowded into my consciousness. Those remembrances hurt, and each one brought about feelings of grief. I had never before experienced such inner pain. Even though engulfed by shame, embarrassment, guilt, and a sense of utter worthlessness, I decided I had to talk to someone. Haltingly, nervously, I told Shirley.

Once she got beyond the initial shock, she said exactly what I needed to hear. "I don't understand this, but I'm with you."

Of course she didn't understand. How could she? I didn't even understand myself.

A few days later, my friend David Morgan came over to my house. I told him as much as I remembered of my past. He held me, and my tears flowed again. I don't recall anything he said, but I knew he was with me in spirit and would be at my side as I slew the dragons of my past.

The Effects of Unconditional Love

Because of the purpose of this book, I want to point out why I think my healing began when it did. Shirley had been the first person in my life who I felt loved me without reservation. I didn't have to be good, act nice, or behave in a particular way to win her acceptance. I had grown up in a family where I was the good boy. I remained the good boy because I did the right things. If I had stopped performing, I was sure the family would hate me. That probably wasn't true, but that's how I felt. Shirley made the difference simply because she loved me. Although it took me a number of years to trust that love, I know I couldn't have faced my childhood assaults if she hadn't been there to encourage me and to hold my hand.

David was the second person who I felt accepted me unconditionally. We had been friends for eight years before my memories began to return. When I tentatively opened up, he didn't push for information or try to fix me. Although I can't explain how, he enabled me to trust him and to share the fragmented memories.

From Shirley and then from David, I slowly began to trust others. I couldn't have done it without that supportive love behind me.

Over the next three years, I shared my abusive childhood with a few others. One of them, Stephen, had led the small group at Oglethorpe. He lived several hundred miles away, but we regularly phoned, wrote, and later e-mailed. Five times, he and I met for a weekend just to talk about our childhoods and to open ourselves to further healing. During those early years, some events were so overpowering, I cried more than I talked. More than once I wished I were dead.

The Cost of Unconditional Love

At the time, I was so filled with my own pain I had no realization of Shirley's pain. She hurt, and had been hurting for years. Whenever one of my odd acts of behavior occurred, she blamed herself for doing something wrong, even if she couldn't figure out what it was. *Both of us were victims of my childhood abuse.*

Once I crept out of the morass, I realized three important facts. First, I was safe and no longer had to fear the terrors of childhood. Second, Shirley understood—as much as anyone who hasn't had the same type of experience could understand. Third—and the most important—Shirley was the first person in my life who had loved me without demands or conditions. Because of her, I had finally found a safe place grounded in reality. When I wanted to deny that the abuse had really happened, she infused me with courage. When I wanted to quit striving for wholeness, Shirley affirmed me by little things, such as holding my hand or letting me see the tears in her own eyes. Shirley's unconditional love enabled me to go through the stages from shame to anger to acceptance, and eventually to forgive my perpetrators, both long dead.

I'm thankful for David's loving friendship, but Shirley was the person I lived with, and the one individual with the most power to hurt me. When I behaved in ways that were not particularly lovable, not once did she reproach me or lash out, and I'm thankful for that. The quality of that love enabled me to accept God's unconditional love. Because of my wife's support, I slowly moved forward until I could say, "I know that God loves me, that I'm worthwhile, loved, and accepted by my heavenly Father."

Through the years, Shirley suffered because of the effects of my abuse. Even now I sometimes feel sad because of the pain she had to go through, especially during those dark years when she had no idea why I behaved as I did. She silently accepted blame and wrestled with her own issues of self-esteem and failure. It was unfair, and I owe her so much for simply sticking with me, for being God's instrument, and most of all for being the human link that joined my hand with that of a loving Father.

3

RANDALL RUSHER'S STORY

Before I presented the keynote address at a writers conference, I sat next to Randall Rusher for the banquet meal. I hadn't met him before, and we began a casual conversation. At one point, he asked, "What are you working on now?"

I mentioned two book projects and said, "And I've just received a contract to write about men who were sexually abused in childhood."

He leaned slightly closer and asked me about the book. I'd been public about my abuse long enough that I sensed he had also been victimized in childhood. I didn't ask, but Randall told me part of his story.

I asked him to write about his experience.

◆　◆　◆

I sat in the courtroom listening to my mother crying and sobbing over the magnitude of the situation. Her son, my brother, was being led in by an armed guard to the table in front of us. Separated from us by a three-foot-high fixed wood barrier and only ten feet of floor space, he might as well have been miles away. His shackled wrists were connected to the chain that circled his waist. He wore the typical red jumpsuit, but the events of this day were anything but typical. Will I ever be able to forget the look of heartbreak on my parents' faces as they saw the eldest of their three sons being led into the courtroom? If that wasn't too much to cope with, they also had to face his heinous crimes. Was this really happening? Could our pasts—my brother's and mine—really have brought our family to this point?

They charged my brother with two counts of child rape and four counts of child molestation. Losing the battle to hold back my own tears, I stared at my family.

This simply can't be happening. Hadn't our family been close? Hadn't we been supportive of each other? On the outside we seemed normal, didn't we? How could we all have been so blinded by denial that we had not seen the symptoms that our childhood sexual abuse had morphed into before they reached such an utterly unbelievable point as this?

My mind felt as if it were splitting in two. I felt deep sadness and loyalty for my brother, and so much sorrow and compassion. I felt even more compassion toward the girls sitting opposite us in the courtroom. After all, I also have daughters of my own only slightly younger. Those girls will have to go into adulthood with injuries that most likely will take decades to heal, if they ever do. *This is so much like the pain my brother and I suffered in our childhood.*

What am I supposed to be feeling? What's normal? Was it really possible to feel so many emotions at the same time? My feelings vacillated between sadness, sorrow, compassion, rage, love, disgust, and empathy.

I wondered what the others on our side of the courtroom were feeling. Or worse yet, what did the mother and the friends and family of the abused girls feel? I could only imagine the rage, the bitterness, the hurt, the utter grief that they must have been experiencing.

So this is where it has led my brother, I thought. The courses our lives took as a result of sexual abuse that he and I went through as children were like those of a river that started at the same headwaters but later divided. Each course contained dangerous rapids along its treacherous journey, but ended up miles apart from each other.

The pain started when I was four years old. In those days I was a boy who loved to play cowboy, and sometimes I climbed onto my mom's lap and soaked up her love.

But one night everything changed. Mom and Dad were out with

friends and my older brother and I were at home with a babysitter. She sexually abused both of us. During the next four years, there were other occurrences from subsequent babysitters and from family friends. Those disgusting memories are etched in my mind forever. No child should have to endure what we suffered because of that babysitter. That initial event changed our lives forever and we could never undo what happened to us.

As the years went by, I no longer looked at my brother in quite the same way. I no longer felt the same sense of love and security as I would climb up into my mom's lap. Had I become broken merchandise? I didn't know what to do about my bad feelings. I was too scared to tell anyone. Who would I tell? I didn't know what, but I thought I had done something wrong. If they knew I had done something wrong, what would they think of me? How would my parents punish me?

Those first years turned into many years of self-condemnation, self-destruction, and ultimately deep despair and depression. My pent-up hurt from the injuries inflicted on me in childhood had become infected and resurfaced many times throughout my adult life.

My emotions surfaced in what I now view as a series of blessings and curses. One of these blessings that manifested itself was an undeniable heartfelt compassion for others, even to the point that at times I felt as though I were actually taking on their pain. My heart truly ached for them and whatever they were going through. That blessing allowed me to interact with people with genuineness and warmth that easily opens a door and authentically builds rapport that seems effortless and safe. People liked me and I liked them.

On the negative side, the injuries were manifested in a curse that played out as an unending longing, craving, and even starving to be accepted by others. I needed a pat on the back, a kind word, and recognition for my achievements. Even the smallest compliments could make my heart sing momentarily. The insatiable need for acceptance and acknowledgment led to ambitious activity.

The harder I worked, the more I was able to please others. The more

I pleased others, the more they acknowledged and accepted me. I studied hard in school and received recognition for my grades. I worked hard in my job and was praised. I exerted myself to build and sustain strong relationships.

I believed that if I were perfect, I would get all the positive strokes I needed to be happy. But it was so difficult to try to be perfect all the time. My self-defeating behavior left me feeling tired, disappointed, anxious, and depressed. Many times, although I worked diligently and sometimes even accomplished amazing things, people didn't respond the way "they were supposed to."

Why didn't they praise my efforts this time? They did before, so why not now? When would I be good enough to be accepted? Good enough to be loved? Good enough to be part of the in-crowd? Yet while trying to succeed in everything I did to experience acceptance, I had to do it in a way that wouldn't hurt anyone. To hurt someone would directly conflict with my heartfelt compassion, kindness, and empathy.

I was in my late twenties when I saw the first signs of the curses beginning to break through the surface in a dramatic and destructive way. I'm not sure whether the money problems, relationships, or drinking came first. It seemed that they all began to hit at about the same time. As I sought after recognition and acceptance by others, I jumped into a series of overly risky business ventures and get-rich-quick schemes that resulted in a long sequence of financial setbacks. But I always believed the next one would be the big one—the financial success that would finally get me the acceptance I longed for.

As each business deal failed and I continued to chase after worldly riches, success, and acceptance, the more my marriage suffered and the more I attempted to dull the pain with drugs and alcohol. While trying to navigate those boiling rapids along the course of my river, I still didn't know or understand the cause of the turbulence.

That part of the river lasted for about six months, in which I lost my wife, my job, wrecked my car, and smoked crack to dull the ever-growing pain. I was days away from losing custody of my two young children and my house. My children were the one thing that kept me from giving up and taking my own life—at least at first.

No one saw the true level of my misery. No single person saw the depths of my struggles. I continued to wear the mask that I had perfected over the years. Everyone saw the nice-guy image. I was the man with a compulsive work ethic, who treated others with respect and kindness and always seemed to wear a smile. I was on guard to let them see only what I wanted them to see.

But I couldn't sustain the facade.

I was too tired to keep up the game. I wanted peace, and I could think of only one way to find it. I had a gun in my hand.

Why am I here? How did I get so messed up? Why am I sad so much of the time? If life has meaning, what is it? Why do I hate my life so much? What good am I?

Those questions and others I'd already asked myself more times than I can remember. But that day I knew I had to resolve them because I could no longer stand the torment that I had struggled with and tried to cope with for the last twenty-nine years.

My life had a drastic change that day while I sat alone in a campground on that typical Northwest fall night. Rain poured down on me, but I didn't care about the cold or the wet. Thoughts and questions filled my heart and mind.

I had decided to end the day by taking my own life. *I'll finally find the peace I've sought.*

As I sat on a large rock in a terrible rain storm, the God of heaven and earth miraculously intervened. I don't recall whether I was crying out to him or not, but as utterly hopeless and desperate as I felt, I most surely was. I had the plan all laid out. I wouldn't leave a note; I didn't know what to say anyway.

My two adorable children could live with their mother. Why not? Wouldn't they be better off without me and my cycles of depression?

I didn't hear voices from God or even feel much of anything as I sat in the campground. Not even the cold mattered as it tried to work its way into my soaked clothes. Nothing mattered except finally finding peace.

Just before I could pull the trigger, I felt an overpowering sense of God's presence. I heard my own voice inside my head say, *I can beat this. I can pull out of my despair.*

I left the campground, and that same day changes began to take place. I had the first feelings of inner peace. I sensed God was with me, even though I didn't understand how. Within three weeks, I had a new job, a car to drive, an apartment to live in, and my children were with me. Most of all, a ray of hope grew inside my heart. I know this type of immediate life change isn't usually how God moves or how he begins the healing process, and I don't try to explain it.

Perhaps it was God who knew I needed something powerful to shake me to the core. Perhaps he had a work for me that hadn't been accomplished. Regardless, I know that the new attitude toward life I received that night in the pouring rain had nothing to do with luck or being in the right place at the right time. It had to do with the tremendous grace and mercy of God Almighty.

I wish I could say that the curses on my life had been miraculously removed, but they didn't disappear. Much healing still needs to occur, but I had received rays of true hope like rays of sunshine warming my skin.

Even up to that point in my life, as strange as it may sound, I struggled accepting that I had been abused. Of course, I was aware that *bad things* had happened to me, but something inside said what happened really wasn't that bad and it wasn't really sexual abuse.

When we were kids, didn't everybody have bad things in their lives? Why should I make a big deal out of mine, especially since so many other kids have had much worse injuries occur to them?

Over the months and years since that night, my eyes have been opened. I now understand how powerful denial can be. I believe recognizing and overcoming denial is the starting gate we have to walk through to find true healing.

Short of a miracle from God, I don't believe that the mental and emotional injuries suffered from sexual abuse can heal to complete restoration. *Healing is not an event but a process—a process that occurs over time.* And time spent seeking God and understanding his genuine, unconditional, unending, and perfect love takes me farther down the healing path.

Another critical aspect of my healing has been the relationship with my wife. Over the past decade, she has been at my side through peaks and valleys. I believe God brought this incredibly strong-willed woman into my life. Without her strength to hold me accountable for my emotions and behavior, my healing would not be as far along as it is.

This hasn't been a painless process. It has felt more like rubbing two rough stones together. At one point in our relationship, the grinding of the stones became so abrasive it looked as though divorce was our only answer.

Again, God intervened in my life. We were separated for several days because both of us felt deeply hurt, and our hearts had hardened toward each other. Yet God miraculously softened them just enough for us to be willing to come together and see a Christian counselor. Because of the magnitude of our past, we needed solid tools to help our relationship heal and to grow. Since then, the rough edges of the stones have become smooth.

As I sat in the courtroom, tears streamed down my face. I heard my brother's voice saying, "I plead guilty."

After a long pause, the judge said, "You are to be confined to a state prison for a period of one-hundred-and-twenty months."

My mind raced. That was *ten years*. He'll be in his mid-fifties by the time he gets released.

How is it that our injuries had been so similar yet the results in our lives so different? He became a perpetrator, the court convicted him, and he's in prison. I'm not a perpetrator, but I realize that I might have become one.

Today I have peace. God had sent me a wife strong enough to endure, a counselor wise enough to coach, a church committed enough to godly teaching. Above all, God remained faithful and loving. I was able to grasp the impact that the childhood abuse had had on my life, to see my past clearly for what it was. Finally seeing that my injuries were real and were terrible and were something that truly happened to me, I no longer had to deny them. But I also realize that the abuse no longer has the power to define me or to keep me in bondage, because I have chosen to pursue total healing.

I have many steps yet to walk in my healing pathway but I'm grateful that I believe the best part of my life, the best days of my life, the best relationships of my life are all yet ahead of me. This gives me reason enough to get up each day with that ray of hope still shining in my heart.

— 4 —

WHERE WAS GOD?

It's the unanswerable question, but it comes up often. Where was God while the abuse took place?

I wasn't a believer until my twenties, so that question didn't trouble me. But many men ask about the absence of divine protection, especially those who were raised in the church. Even more by those who were victimized by pastors, Sunday school teachers, elders, or other church leaders.

"Where was God?" they ask. "How could church leaders do such things?"

I start by quoting James 3:1, which urges, "Dear brothers and sisters, not many of you should become teachers in the church, for we who teach will be judged more strictly." The verse refers to *teacher* as an office within the church, but I think it's fair to apply the verse to anyone in a responsible position who teaches others in the church directly or indirectly by lifestyle.

The point is that on the day of final judgment, God *will* judge them more severely. When they take on a teaching or leadership role, they claim to know the right from the wrong and cling to the right. Others may falter—and we all do—but by accepting a leadership position, they hold themselves up as those we should follow and imitate.

What I've just written probably doesn't bring much comfort to someone who was molested by a trusted leader of the church, but it is a divine promise of justice.

Second, I don't know why God doesn't shield the young from terrible experiences. I don't know why some depraved human beings are so driven by their own lusts and desires that they have no compassion for the innocent, especially children. Where was God? It's the same question that others have asked for centuries: Why do bad things happen to good people?

I don't know the answer.

I don't know anyone who does; however, I do know God.

Because I'm a serious Christian, I believe in a loving, compassionate, and caring God. Isaiah 55:8 tells us that our ways aren't his and his ways are beyond us. God rebuked Job for trying to act as if he knew all the answers.

But I have found one answer that satisfies me.

In 2007, our house burned to the ground. My son-in-law died in the fire, and we lost everything. A few weeks after the fire, a Jewish friend in Florida heard about the fire and called me.

I gave him details and he kept saying, "You're a good man. You don't deserve this."

I didn't respond. *Who does deserve it?* I asked silently. My friend was disturbed, and his anguish was meant to comfort me. Finally he said, "You're a man of God, Cec. Where was God in all this?"

A response came to me immediately—not an original one—but an answer that made me know it was correct. "Where was God?" I repeated. "He was at the same place he was when his own Son died."

My friend didn't speak for a few seconds. "Does that satisfy you? Does that bring you comfort?"

"It does."

He mumbled something about the need for justice and moved on to something else. That was all right because I sensed his discomfort.

Even if I knew *why* God hadn't intervened in the fire or in my abuse, would it make any difference? Would it make me feel better? It still happened. The sexual assault took place, and one day the perpetrators will have to stand before God for their sins. In the meantime, I find comfort in reminding myself that God doesn't promise to protect me from evil. He does promise to be with me when I encounter evil.

5

A THEFT OF CHILDHOOD

"How can you talk about the loss of childhood?" he challenged. "How can you lose something you never had?" He raged about never being able to feel or to behave like a child. "I spent my early *years* satisfying my mother's emotional needs and my dad's sexual impulses."

He was one of the men in the state-sponsored group in which I participated for a year. I don't remember his name but I vividly remember his anger.

He wasn't the only one who felt that way, but he was the most volatile. Most of us who have been sexually assaulted feel that way. I've sometimes said, "I never had a childhood." What that means is, for us, the trauma of the abuse obliterated the good things about those early years.

Until I dealt with my abuse, I had no memories of my home life before I was eleven years old. And yet I had many clear memories of school. I clearly recalled the day my oldest sister and her husband took me to second grade in a new school building. Despite that, I was cut off from the emotions, the freedom, and carefree life that we assume all children have or are entitled to have.

From television, especially the sitcoms, we watch the images of families interacting and being happy, and the children receiving an abundance of love. Even if an evil witch, malevolent uncle, or disagreeable grandparent lurks about, someone reaches out to the children, protects them, and loves them.

If only life could have been that good for those of us who were molested. Reality for us was different. Even for kids who had the best of childhoods life didn't fit the sitcom ideal. All kids have to learn about the world and how to fit into it. In our early years, we absorb the reality that every adult has the right to criticize, discipline, or correct us. We've all likely been told at one time, "This is for your own good." Because of that built-in understanding, many of us didn't know how to refuse the demands of an adult. That was especially true when the adult said, "This is our secret. Don't tell anyone."

So what were the formative years like for abused children? I can tell you how I used to answer that question. After I grew up and before I dealt with my issues, people sometimes asked about my childhood. "Conventional home," I'd say. "My dad was quiet and not demonstrative but my mother was warm." I lied, but I didn't know it was a lie. I couldn't remember our home life, and the words I spoke seemed correct. It was fortunate that no one ever probed beyond that initial statement. Since I had no memories of abuse or pain, I assumed that my childhood must have been normal and enjoyable.

I said that my dad was quiet—that was true. Only years later was I able to add, ". . . except every weekend. That's when he got drunk and that's when the beatings occurred." I didn't remember the physical beatings until I remembered the sexual assault.

I was fifty years old, and had dealt with many of my childhood issues, before it hit me—my mom wasn't warm. She was emotionally detached. I was a demonstrative kid, and I initiated the hugs. That was a revelation for me. I thought about her a long time. She cried easily, but the tears were for herself.

One day I said to Shirley, "My mother wasn't warm and loving."

Shirley stared at me in unbelief. "Whoever said she was? I always thought she was a cold person."

I hadn't ever questioned my perception of my mother. Until I recaptured the memories of the past, I had no reference to my home life. The memories and the pain didn't torment me, but they influenced most of my decisions. It took me a long time to understand how the abuse affected me.

Stages of Abuse

Some have listed the phases of abuse a boy goes through. They're fairly obvious, but I want to state them here.

First, he is attracted to the aggressor. The adult reaches out to the boy. To a neglected boy or one who feels unwanted or unimportant, that attraction can be powerful.

Second, the adult seduces the boy. The boy relishes the attention and it makes him feel special. In fact, that's a common term we abused kids heard from perpetrators: "You're special." The boys sometimes perceive the abuse as what they must pay for the attention and affection they receive. They don't have the maturity to reason that they have been deceived or that they are merely the object of someone's lust.

Third, the boy tries to adapt to the situation. He may hate what's being done to him, but in the process he is held, kissed, and touched. Like all human creatures, he has a natural, inborn skin hunger and he responds. With his immature reasoning ability, he tries to explain to himself how this can be good and tolerable even if it's wrong and unbearable.

Fourth, the abuse ends. If the aggressor is a true pedophile he may not like it when the boy reaches a certain age, such as when he grows pubic hair. Even if the boy doesn't tell anyone, the day comes when the molester, fixated on children, abruptly leaves the boy.

The leaving, or the child's being pushed away, can be almost as traumatic to the boy as the abuse itself. *Why doesn't he love me anymore? What did I do wrong?* In some ways the boy is worse off than before the molestation. Earlier, he felt alone and unloved. Now he adds to that feelings of guilt for doing something wrong—even though he doesn't grasp what it is.

Some of those boys may move into prostitution or become abusers themselves. Most of them, like me, end up confused and uncertain about life.

The Losses We Suffer

Even if we don't retain the memories of abuse, our lives can still be warped and filled with pain. We abused kids suffered, and we endure many losses.

Loss of Memory

I've already mentioned loss of memory. One way some of us survive the pain is to forget it or push it out of our consciousness. If we have to deny or forget what was done to us so we can survive childhood, we may grow up, look back, and ask, "Where was my childhood?" To be deprived of the memories—even the good ones—is abuse. And when we begin to recover our memories, we also understand why we "forgot."

In one group meeting, we talked about our amnesia, and one man spoke up. "Now it makes sense!" He said that the only thing he had remembered about childhood was that he seemed always to be alone. "Now I understand that being alone was when I felt safe. There was no one around to hurt me."

Loss of Control

In childhood, children learn to differentiate between what belongs to them and what doesn't. The most intimate possession is our bodies. Sexual molestation violates our ultimate sense of self. Someone else takes control of our bodies—against our wills.

Because we are children, we don't feel we have the right to protect ourselves from attack, or we don't know how. An adult, an authority figure, violates us. And as children, we "learned" that adults didn't hurt kids.

Many molested children also learned that the world isn't a safe place and they had to protect themselves. For many, though, the loss of control over our bodies robbed us of the normal ability to protect ourselves. To compensate, some men stay in the victim mind-set all their lives, rebel-ling and fighting anyone who tries to get close. On the other end of the spectrum are men who become revictimized, remaining naive or unaware of the evil intentions of others, and who end up being taken advantage of.

Even after we grew up and became physically larger, many of us felt small and helpless. That's the pattern we learned as children. When we looked into mirrors we often saw ourselves as ugly and unattractive—regardless of the reality.

Despite any evidence, we accepted the lies that sexual abuse taught us. We were lied to—and not only in words but in actions. We were lied to about love. We were lied to about caring. We became objects of some-one else's lust. For many, to be loved meant to have a sexual experience. Is it any wonder that some adult survivors can't distinguish between making love and having sex?

During my early recovery, I spoke with a man who probably would be classified as morbidly obese. One night he said, "By getting fat and look-ing ugly, no one wanted to hurt me. They left me alone." He told me his neighbor molested him repeatedly until he became a teen. "That's when I put on pounds—a lot of pounds." One day the neighbor said to him, "You're disgusting and fat." He never touched the boy again. "And now I'm more than a hundred pounds overweight, and I can't get rid of my protective coating."

Other adult survivors become controlling, demanding, and inflexible. Some become addicted to sex with women as a way to prove to them-selves and to others that they aren't homosexuals. Many are suspicious of everyone. How can they trust anyone when their natural ability to trust was stolen during childhood?

Loss of Nurture

A third serious loss—and there are many others—is the loss of a healthy, nurturing environment. Children deserve to be loved. We can't protect them from falling when they start to walk or from fumbling the first time they try to catch a ball. But shouldn't they have—and don't they deserve to have—an atmosphere of acceptance and love?

Children need to know that they are wanted and that they are loved. They also need to know that no matter how bad the world is, they have families to protect them. This isn't to blame parents for the abuse of their children by someone else. It is to point out again the loss that abused kids feel. When kids can't feel protected and safe, they've lost something that they can never regain. Because of not being loved and valued as children, it's difficult for them as adults to create a sense of healthy self-esteem and worth.

One of my sisters told me that when I was about four years old, every chance I had I ran to a neighbor's house and often stayed for the evening meal. (I don't remember that.) I believe it was my attempt to compensate for my loss of childhood and family by finding a substitute. As I grew older, probably about twelve, I hated to go home and stayed away as much as possible. By the time I was fourteen, home was the place only to sleep and get my clothes washed.

My friends liked to go home and often invited me. Only one time during those years do I remember inviting a friend to our house—and we didn't stay long.

One of the big fallouts of lost childhoods is that the boys may feel that the only place they can find love and intimacy is with those people who abuse them. Clark said that he had many homosexual experiences up through his early twenties. "I needed to be held, and I yearned to have someone say, 'I love you.' And it worked." He wasn't gay, but he said it was the only way he had ever received affection from a man. Of course, that wasn't affection, but it took Clark a long time to understand the difference.

Emotional Responses

Think about the man in your life who was assaulted. He may have times when he feels nothing; he may have periods when he screams or cries. At one point in my recovery, I cried every day and wondered if I would ever stop.

"Maybe they're stored up tears for yourself," another survivor told me. "Maybe you're now crying for yourself because you couldn't do it as a child."

I think he is correct.

Over time I was glad I was able to cry. I met men who couldn't—who wouldn't give in. A man in one group said he'd forgotten how to cry. I believed him. He said everything in a monotone. He seemed unable to open up to his emotions and feel his own pain.

As survivors we tried to support him. He observed some of us crying and one time he said to me, "You're much healthier than you were when you first came."

The moistness in his eyes told me something had changed. "So are you," I said.

He shook his head. Finally he said, "Maybe a little."

He also became a dropout from that group. He, along with ten others, dropped out during the year. I believe several of them were afraid to experience their emotions. They seemed to fear that once they began to re-experience the pain, they wouldn't be able to stop.

I understood, and I'd had similar feelings. I finally figured out, though, that because the abuse took place in childhood, a portion of what I felt was similar to how I'd experienced emotions as a child. The emotions of children are more frightening to them because they accept everything as true or false, white or black. I had to learn to live through those child-sized emotions, which frightened me more than adult-sized ones. For the first thirty-five years of my life I tended to see everything as an ultimate decision or a decided tragedy. Everything was life-or-death. As a child, that's also how I saw life. Every bad situation appeared so serious that I was sure my decision determined eternal consequences. That sounds absurd now, but like many assault survivors, I saw only the *now* and all decisions determined destiny.

We survivors of sexual abuse need not only emotional and physical healing, we need to embrace the spiritual aspect of recovery. As a Christian, one of the most helpful things to me was to continue to read about God's love in the Bible. It wasn't easy for me to acknowledge that I'm lovable simply because God created me. But, as they said a generation ago, "God don't make no junk" and "God don't make ugly."

6

"THAT WAS THE PAST"

If the man in your life is going to recover, he must face his past. For him, the past was a time of pain and confusion. It won't be easy for him to venture there, but I don't know any way to live happily in the present until the pain of the past has been overcome.

Forgetting, Denying, and Ignoring the Past

Too many male survivors want to say, "It doesn't do any good to talk about things that happened in childhood. I want to move forward, not go into all of that." They want to believe that the passage of time has erased the effects of their childhood pain. What they often don't realize is that they have remained chained by the horrific events, and the abuse still influences their present attitudes and actions.

Almost every man I've met who spoke of abuse also talked about feelings of insecurity and inadequacy. Some of them had been involved in risky behavior, and others struggled with forms of addiction. Thomas Edward says, "The struggle to break this pattern is often useless because the past which created it is ignored."[1]

The adult survivor needs to understand what happened and, perhaps even more important, realize why his childhood survival modes deter his present growth. Ignoring those issues—as if he could—or the thoughts and feelings he's probably pushed aside doesn't make them go

1. Thomas Edward, *Healing a Man's Heart* (Seattle: Holy Fire Publishing, 2009), 7.

away. As one friend said it, "The only way out [of the pain] is to knock on the door of pain, go inside, and feel the emotions. If he does that, the past will no longer hurt him."

Dann Youle of Land Office Ministries says that when he talks to men about their abusive past, he first assesses whether they're ready to hear what he wants to say. Too often they want a quick fix, a Band-Aid response. If, however, he senses they will listen, he says, "If you keep this secret in the dark, it works like cancer that spreads throughout your system. Until you do something about it, the cancer continues to grow."

Refusal to look backward has its consequences. The past becomes the proverbial elephant in the room—everyone knows it's present but chooses to ignore it. Not to deal with the past damages relationships and hinders a man from living the abundant life Jesus promised his disciples.

My youngest brother, Chuck, for example, acknowledged he'd been molested, but he insisted, "That happened when I was a kid. It doesn't do any good to go back and talk about all of that old stuff."

When I pushed him, he reminded me that the woman who abused both of us was dead. "There's nothing we can do about it."

"We can find resolution," I said.

"I'm fine." He lit a cigarette and turned away from me while he opened his third can of beer during the half hour we'd been talking.

Despite two conversations, Chuck refused to talk about the past. He admitted, reluctantly, that one reason he drank was, "It's the only time I don't feel rotten." On the few occasions when I tried to talk to him, his answers were (1) "You can't undo the past," (2) "We don't have to think about those things," or (3) "That stuff happened back then." His words implied that we need only to forget the past, leave it behind, and it's gone.

If only it were that simple. On rare occasions when he was drunk, he made oblique references to "that mess in childhood." Outwardly, Chuck wanted to get past the sexual assault and get on with his life. I wish he'd been able to let go of the past. He died from his daily, thirty-year-long medication called alcohol.

My younger brother, Mel, an alcoholic since his teens, was married five times and died of cirrhosis at age forty-eight. Unlike Chuck, Mel wouldn't even acknowledge the experiences of our childhood. "There's nothing back there I want to talk about," was the most he said.

I write about my two brothers because both of them seemed determined to get past the abuse of childhood by forgetting, denying, or ignoring it. That approach doesn't work. It certainly didn't work for either of them.

We don't forget—not really. We may not remember everything, but we can't erase the worst traumas by an act of the will. We don't forget, because childhood abuse shapes our attitudes about ourselves and others and involves all our relationships. Some men want to hurry and get over the past, but it's not something to get over.

Remembering, Accepting, and Facing the Past

Abuse happened to us and, since you're reading this book, probably to a man you love very much. Until he accepts and faces what it's done to mess up his life, he can't move forward. He can only live an unhealed life.

"You might be done with the past," Robert once said to me, "but the past isn't ever done with you." He began going to therapy because of other issues in his life, unaware that they stemmed from his childhood assault. During therapy, he brought up his abuse himself and spoke about it matter-of-factly, as if it had happened to someone else. "I felt proud of the fact that I could talk about it so easily," he said.

When his therapist asked, "How do you feel?" Robert drew a blank. He had dissociated himself from his emotions. It took months of twice-weekly visits before he learned to trust his therapist. Once they had established a relationship, and Robert felt he could open up, he was able to examine his childhood and to start moving toward healing.

You may not clearly understand the effects when the past clings to a man who was abused as a child or the implications it has for him to ignore or deny his abusive childhood. To clarify how the past intrudes on the unhealed present, here are two examples. Although the first illustration involves a small, seemingly insignificant intrusion, the principle is valid.

I'm not a fussy eater and I have few food preferences. That's important to point out. During the six years we spent in Kenya, a number of missionaries met with us for an annual convention in a remote area called Suna, where we lived. We ate our meals together. During the first convention, a missionary brought several jars of raspberry jam—we call it preserves in the United States—for us to eat each afternoon with our homemade bread and tea.

I stared at the jam and my stomach revolted. "Did you bring any other kind?"

"Everyone likes raspberry jam," she said, "so that's all I brought."

I absolutely couldn't eat the jam. I didn't make any comment about it, but for three days I ate only butter on my bread. It didn't make sense to me because I'm fond of raspberries—or any kind of fruit. I even remembered from my childhood a large jar, perhaps pint-sized, of raspberry jam. I could even see the store label on the jar. But I absolutely couldn't eat the jam. Each time I looked at the raspberry jam, I felt slightly nauseated. At the next year's convention, I made sure we had strawberry and peach jams as well.

I never did say anything to Shirley or to anyone else, but after that incident I often wondered why I detested raspberry jam. After I began to deal with my abuse, I realized why raspberry jam nauseated me. When I was a boy, an elderly man rented one room in our house. The old man, Mr. Lee, used to entice me into his room by giving me crackers with jam—raspberry jam.

Years later I talked to one of my sisters about Mr. Lee and brought up his feeding us crackers and raspberry jam. She had forgotten about the snack, but as I mentioned it, she said, "You know, that's right. I hadn't thought of that for years."

Although I had long "forgotten" the abuse, the dislike of raspberry jam was associated with my molestation. My point is that even if we outwardly forget or push away the events, something deep inside still remembers. Such memories aren't always as benign as the jam example.

The second illustration came from a man whom everyone called Red—for obvious reasons. Red had a fairly normal adjustment. He never forgot his abuse, but he did forget his abuser, a man who lived across the street. Red mentioned that all through his life, he hated men with handlebar mustaches. "You can't trust them—not any of them," he said more than once. If a man with a handlebar mustache came around, Red walked away or refused to talk to him. Red insisted that they were sneaky and mean-spirited. Despite his friends' laughing at him, Red insisted that anyone with a handlebar mustache couldn't be trusted.

One Christmas season Red visited his childhood home in Alabama, where his parents still lived. One evening they sat around and looked at childhood pictures. At some point his mother said, "I don't suppose you remember . . ." and she mentioned the name of the neighbor who had sexually abused Red—and he hadn't told his family about the abuse. She held up a picture of the man holding seven-year-old Red in his arms. The man wore a handlebar mustache.

Red stared at the photograph, stood up abruptly, and rushed into the bathroom. He vomited into the toilet.

These are two true, simple stories, but they illustrate that the past isn't dead just because it's the past and just because we don't remember the actual events. Until the victimized man in your life faces his abusive past, it's still with him. He may not recall events, but his stomach remembers what his head forgets.

Today, few therapists believe that memories are stored totally intact, but they do accept that certain significant events stay with us. If they're painful or negative, memories of them might be sublimated, as in Red's case and mine.

If such mundane things as jam or facial hair triggered strong emotional responses, doesn't that suggest something? It is necessary, then, to focus on the past in order to uncover the motivations, the emotions, and the traumas that lie under years of attempting to forget.

For the man you love, facing his past isn't easy, and it *is* painful. But victorious survivors have to go through the darkness to enter into the light of the abundant life that Jesus Christ promised. The memories, regardless of how fragmentary, still torment. Torment means pain, and pain hurts.

Opening himself to the past might be one of the hardest things he'll ever attempt. It may also be one of the bravest. It's not an easy journey and there's no miraculous prayer or potent drug he can take. He's probably already tried some forms of self-medication and they didn't work. The reality is, he can't fully live in the present until he no longer hides from his past. As long as those memories torture him, they hold him back from experiencing the fullness of life.

Twelve-step programs, such as the one patterned after Alcoholics Anonymous (AA), stress that for anyone to recover, that person must admit to being powerless and give up the illusion of being in control. The principle applies to victims of molestation as well.

Think of it this way. The adult survivor has lived with pain and confusion since childhood. He probably has tried a variety of ways to numb himself. Whenever emotions overwhelmed my friend Robert, he numbed out and felt nothing. Others—and the man in your life might be one of them—deaden their pain through food, work, alcohol, pornography, drugs, or some other form of addiction. Still others join a variety of church or religious orders, secretly looking for the magic formula to set them free. Some try to escape geographically by moving from place to place.

There's one serious problem with those solutions: *They don't work.* I can cite many examples of bizarre behavior and self-destructive patterns aimed at covering the old wounds, but they all point to the same end: they won't heal him. Whatever strategies he used to help him feel better, to endure, to survive, or just to fit in may have helped. They had a purpose in alleviating unbearable pain. He survived, but he didn't thrive.

Many a man in the recovery process says, "I used to feel that pieces of me were missing." He says that, though, only when he begins to feel the missing pieces being restored.

The man you love needs to be ready to face the past. When he's ready—or as survivors often say—"When I feel safe, I can deal with it."

Dann Youle says that he taught the manual called *Living Waters*—a program of Desert Stream Ministries in Kansas City, Missouri—at least three times before the message hit him: "I was abused."

Dann also said, "The Lord never forces you, but waits until you're ready. When Christians don't want to deal with an issue, the Holy Spirit will later put them in the right circumstances to bring the problem into the open. Why not face the pain once instead of going through it four or five times?"

For him to encounter his past brings up pain that he may not want to experience again, but confronting the horrendous past offers victory and healing in the present. He can't skip the pain.

By his recalling his past, the healing journey begins. He may remember the fact of abuse but little or nothing else. He may have specific memories. Or perhaps he can remember only his feelings at the time the molestation took place. No matter what kind of memories, that's a good place to start.

+   +   +

As he begins the healing process, he'll encounter problems that will slow him down, maybe even stop him temporarily or permanently. He'll handle only as much as he can at one time. He may feel overwhelmed by emotions, confusion, shock, shame, and guilt. Depression may tug at him. Flashbacks or anxiety attacks can torment him, and his dreams may turn into nightmares. He might be tempted to lapse into denial or blame himself for the evil done to him.

When I began to deal with the effects of my childhood abuse, it took me almost ten years before I could honestly say, "The pain is gone." The worst part of the pain, however, took place during the first year. We all heal at different speeds.

As a man becomes aware of the reservoir of emotions within him, he may feel and express sadness, anger, hurt—emotions that have lain dormant for years. He may fear he'll lose control or go crazy. He may ask, "Will I ever feel good again?" He's not asking for a yes or no answer. He's asking for you to stand by him and see him through his struggle.

He has to walk through "the valley of the shadow of death" to reach the mount of jubilation. While he's doing so, he might be trying to take care of *you*, worried that you won't be able to handle his pain and trauma. As he becomes more comfortable with the painful feelings and equally aware that you are able to accept the difficulty of his healing process, he can accept the past. He'll also realize that the feelings gradually decrease in intensity. When I went through the most painful part of my healing, for weeks every experience was so intense I kept saying, "If I could only turn off the pain."

I also felt some shame and guilt after I told Shirley and David about my abuse. I realize that shame and guilt are emotions and they're not logical, but emotions don't listen to logic. Shame is a deep sense of feeling bad or evil. The old man who abused me used to bribe me with jam and crackers and say, "This is our secret." Some men report that they were told, "If you tell anyone, I won't want to have anything to do with you, and no one else will love you."

Guilt is related to shame. For me it came from feeling that in some way I'd been responsible for the abuse—even though I couldn't explain how. Questions about self-blame and guilt tugged at me. Some part of me insisted that it had been my fault or that I had caused the abuse. Logic said that a five-year-old boy didn't seduce a man in his late sixties, but I still focused on what I called my raw emotions.

I also decided that no matter how bad I felt, I had to move forward. Shame wouldn't hold me back. I was fortunate in that I didn't live with any of my surviving siblings, and my parents were dead. Some men are afraid to upset family members so they hold back.

"I was afraid they would get upset if I brought it up," Ronnie said to me.

"So it's better for you to remain in pain than to upset the family dynamic?" I asked. "What about *your* feelings? When do they count?"

We talked for perhaps half an hour before Ronnie said he had to decide whether his feelings were at least as important as those of the rest of the family. It was a difficult, painful decision, but about a week later he decided to tell other family members. It was the past, but the past obscured the joy of the present.

Two years later Ronnie and I ran into each other at a conference. He thanked me for pushing him. "After you asked me if my feelings counted, I realized they did. When I was growing up, I was the one who kept things calm and brought peace among my siblings. Now it was my turn to let the family calm me down."

We hugged and shed a few tears. I was near the end of my painful journey; Ronnie was in the middle of his. But we were both on the journey.

7

FLASHBACKS AND DREAMS

Flashbacks are intrusive memories about the abuse. They can frighten us or confuse us. Once we realize flashbacks are part of the healing process, we learn to accept them. Flashbacks might, in fact, be a healthy sign. Having them says that the complicated psyche is free enough to open the door, however slightly; that a man is more psychologically and spiritually ready to move forward in healing.

Flashbacks, sometimes called re-experiencing, are extremely common in the healing process. We can't control the flashbacks and we never know when they'll come. Something triggers the physical, visual, olfactory, or auditory memory. A billboard, a snatch of music, or even a house can trigger a flashback.

One may come at an extremely intimate moment. A man told me that one night he and his wife were in bed and were holding and kissing each other. She touched the back of his neck and he jumped out of bed and yelled, "Don't ever do that again!" She stared at him and began to cry.

His mind had flashed back—re-experienced—the way his priest had touched him when he pulled him close. Someone else said that one night he couldn't kiss his wife because of the smell of the toothpaste she used. She hadn't bought that brand before but he remembered it as the smell and taste of his abuser's mouth.

Flashbacks are just that—they're a flash—a quick moment when victims return to the past, and they are common to those of us who have been sexually assaulted. They appear as memories or fragments of memories from past events. They can be jarring, painful, and often disruptive. Some last a few seconds, but men have reported flashbacks as lasting longer and involving extensive memory recall. Those are usually more powerful. We can't predict when they'll come—day or night—but they always take us by surprise. Sometimes flashbacks replay events that we had long forgotten.

Flashbacks seem more common in what we call the first person. That is, the person re-experiences an event. Mine were usually in the third person. That is, I seemed to stand in a room and watch while things happened. I could see that I was the person, but I seemed to be observing it rather than feeling it myself.

Occasionally, survivors feel as though they are actually back in that time and place. They experience the trauma again. In those moments, they often relive the past experiences as though they were happening all over again.

Flashbacks can take many forms. They can be *visual memories*: images, three-dimensional Technicolor images, or black and white. Most of my flashbacks were blurry—clear enough for me to recognize and remember, but I couldn't see faces clearly. They might be feeling memories—no actual images. Your loved one may not remember specific events, but he still holds the feelings that went along with that experience.

One time I was in a group and someone rubbed the top of my hand and just above my wrist. I pulled back, startled, and wanted to run. I'm not sure why the person did that, but it brought back a feeling from childhood. That's how Mr. Lee started the abuse: a gentle rubbing of my arm. "You have smooth skin," he would often say.

Auditory memories can be sounds like music or deep breathing. A man can suffer a flashback when he hears footsteps or when a door opens in the middle of the night.

Sensory memories happen with certain smells, like perfume or body odor. I met a man who couldn't stand the smell of Dentyne chewing gum. That was the bribe his perpetrator used.

Body memories show up by such things as nausea, suffocating, gagging, or difficulty swallowing. I was in a group in Seattle years ago and one man spoke about his fear of being held down. When he entered high school he wanted to play football but freaked out when he was tackled. Something about the physical sensations reminded him of painful experiences as a child.

A man might have emotional memories—feelings of distress, hopelessness, rage, terror, dread, danger, or an emotional numbing out. Other men talked of experiencing frequent headaches, blurred vision, or floating sensations.

We can't control when we'll have flashbacks, but we can control what we'll do with them. If a man accepts the memory as part of his life experience, it's less likely to bother him again or at least less seriously. The pain of the flashbacks usually makes him say, "I wish it had never happened."

"It's the surprise," Jake said. "They can come out of nowhere. They keep getting in the way of my living my life."

To help us get on with our lives might be one reason for such flashbacks. The actual experiences were so horrendous that we pushed them out of our conscious minds. They took up permanent residence in some unknown cavern of our psyche, and they'll stay there and may continue to haunt us until we're able to acknowledge them.

Once we as adults acknowledge those experiences, flashbacks lose their power to disturb or frighten us. Instead of hurrying to rid myself of flashbacks, I learned to see them as healing tools. I began to say to myself, *God sent them to me. They've come to help me get rid of the pain I couldn't handle as a child.* As simple as those words sound, it worked for me, and I accepted them as God's message to me that said, "Here is one more painful experience you pushed away. I've sent it back to you at this time so you can admit it, cope with it, and move on to the next step in your life."

Some advocate writing down the flashbacks. I didn't, and I felt no need to do so. Writing can be helpful if a memory fragment arises and the man can't place it or remember the context. One man, for instance, had the flashback of a curtain pulled back and a large, monstrous-sized hand grabbing his genitals. That flashback came to him three times in a single week before he was able to put it together. As a Boy Scout, he'd been on a camping trip. The hand was that of his scoutmaster coming into his tent. As he told us the story he said, "I never told anyone. Who would believe me? Everyone admired him, and he was one of those pillars that held up the community."

◆   ◆   ◆

What applies to flashbacks also applies with dreams. They come beyond our control. They help our healing if we're ready to accept them. For as long as I could remember, I had a recurring dream, but I became aware of its prevalence only a year or so after Shirley and I married. It occurred maybe twenty times in a year, and it was always the same dream.

It took place in the house I grew up in—what had once been a duplex. The house was a wooden structure painted white, with five front steps, and a mailbox on either side of the door. In my dream I walked up those five steps. Most of the time, I'd see a letter in one of the mailboxes, and I knew it was addressed to me. As I would stare at it, I realized we hadn't lived there since I was in eleventh grade. It amazed me that the letter would be in the box, waiting for me all those years. I never picked up the letter, but I put my hand on the door handle to go inside and the dream ended. I wondered why I couldn't get into the house.

Once I began my recovery, I had the dream more regularly—sometimes four times a week. Because that recurring dream had been such a part of my life I hadn't connected it to my abuse. After I was past the worst part of my trauma, the dream changed. There was no longer a letter in the mailbox. I opened the door and went inside.

In my dreams over the next few months, I explored the house. The first time, I walked inside and stood in the front hallway. A few times I went to the door on the right—my parents' bedroom—or sometimes went to the door on the left, which was the room that Mr. Lee rented from us.

For a time one thing confused me. I could see only the lower half of the room. One morning when I thought about the dream and connected it to my abuse, I thought, *Of course. I was a kid then. That would have been all I could have seen.*

The next night I dreamed I went into the kitchen and sat in my favorite spot. My mother cooked on a stove that sat on four legs, high off the floor. She often had boxes in the empty space, but I sometimes pushed them together and sat under the stove. No one paid much attention to me when I sat there. I dreamed I was there, and I saw the kitchen as I'd seen it hundreds of times in my childhood.

About a month passed before I realized something: the dream had stopped coming to me. It had been so familiar to me I hadn't questioned it. But once the healing reached a certain stage, apparently I no longer needed the dream. It hasn't returned since then.

I now realize that dreams provide valuable information about our feelings, thoughts, and attitudes. They often come disguised or in symbols, but if we can be receptive, they help us understand our world and become invaluable.

I shared my dreams in a men's group, and Randy began to cry. He didn't want to talk to anyone and we left him alone. After the meeting, he came to me and hugged me. His tears flowed again. "I had a dream—several times. I was in a pool of water—at first I thought it was one of those kids' wading pools. A man kept chasing me around the pool."

I wasn't sure where the dream was going so I said nothing and listened.

"Tonight as you spoke, I realized that it wasn't a pool—it was a bathtub. And the man was my father."

That was Randy's clearest memory of the abuse. Once he connected his dad and the tub, other dreams came and so did flashbacks.

"Before the healing, comes the pain," he said softly.

After the first months of my healing journey, I became thankful for flashbacks and dreams. They encouraged me to know that I was ready to be healed and that God was leading me forward.

8

FALSE MEMORIES?

"Why do we want to remember?" one of my brothers asked.

The simple answer is that it's part of the healing process. We have to face the problem before we can begin to deal with it.

For a long time I assumed my inability to remember was unique. It is currently estimated that as many as 50 percent of men don't remember their molestation until years afterward. As with me, something in adulthood has to trigger the memories.

Why did I remember when I did? I don't know. My guess is that I was at the place in my life where I was open. I had been a pastor for fourteen years, and I focused on others and their problems. About a year after I resigned to write full-time, I was able to focus on myself. I'm also convinced that, along with the new career, my longtime habit of running triggered my memories.

Running is a mindless sport, and the repetitive motion became a marvelous way for me to focus on God. I spent most of my praying time on the hoof. I didn't listen to a radio or tapes because I wanted that time to be special and reserved for God. For me, the repetitive running pattern opened the way to my past. I was able to remember many things, although I still have gaps and vague memories.

Some men regain even less. "I can't recall most of what happened," one man said to me, "but I know who did it and what he did."

I've learned that those of us who repressed our memories did so because the pain was too overwhelming. It was our method of being able to survive. The alternative would have been to feel the pain each day. As

I look back, I realize that denial or loss of memory was God's kindness to get me through childhood.

For years friends spoke of their childhoods, and I'd smile and think, *That's what they've been told by someone else. They don't really remember.* In my case, I remembered nothing that happened at home before the summer I entered sixth grade.

It's a strange memory because it contradicted other things in my life. Like many men with repressed memories, we tell people we had a conventional childhood. My first memory, the one I carried deep inside, didn't make sense to me. Until the door of closed memory opened, I couldn't connect with it.

I was in our back yard, behind a huge elm tree. I had carried the sharp butcher knife from the kitchen. I planned to kill myself by plunging it into my stomach and twisting it, like I'd seen done in a movie. As I sat there, lifted my shirt, and held the knife against my stomach, I thought, *No one will miss me. Mom might cry, but there are so many of us, she'll soon forget.*

I stared at the knife for a long time before I realized I couldn't go through with it. I yelled at myself, even called myself a coward. I threw down the knife and used every word of profanity I knew, but I couldn't plunge that knife into my stomach.

It's an isolated memory but I used to wonder why I wanted to take my life when I had a normal, happy childhood. It didn't make sense—then.

Those Memories

When the memories return, the healing can start, but dealing with the pain isn't easy. For many of us, with the return of memory the pain, in fact, increases. We re-experience the hurt that we experienced in childhood. For me, at least, I struggled with those half-remembered events.

Did it really happen? Have I made it up?

Most of us molested males have asked that question. There's a difference, though, between repressed memories and what is now called *false memory syndrome*. False memory syndrome implies that, consciously or not, someone (usually a therapist) has influenced another's memory of the past by questions or statements that evoke events or images. Those words distort, or create a false memory.

It's helped me to realize that memory isn't a videotape of the past. We don't deposit past events in a subterranean vault until they're ready to be retrieved. To some degree, memory is *a reconstruction of the past*. It's susceptible to bias and error. It's a mistake, then, to consider that our memories are intact.

When it comes to important details, the man in your life needs to realize that he will have forgotten them or misconstrued them. He'll probably never retrieve everything. But he will, and often does, relive the emotions. In the meantime, we men can only do our best to reconstruct the past, and we have to realize that it's only a partial reconstruction.

Despite that, memories are important. What stays with survivors of sexual assault—as incomplete as the recollections might be—is that they are enabled to grasp how life was then and to compare it with the present. Those snatches from the past enable them to understand some of the strange feelings they have now.

"I'm heterosexual and I'm sure about that," Rog told me. "But one thing troubles me. When I see a man with chest hair protruding over the top of his undershirt, I have a compulsion to touch it." He looked at me and asked, "Is that weird?"

I asked him to tell me about his abuser. It had been a neighbor. He came over the first time during a hot summer and he wore one of those sleeveless undershirts. His chest hair was exposed, and he started the abuse by taking Rog's hand and making him feel the hair.

"Makes sense to me," I said.

As we talked, Rog realized that he hated doing it, but the perpetrator made him do it every time.

What Are False Memories?

Some memories are distorted through influences such as taking in new information. I've observed this sort of altering in the conversion stories of many Christians. In the early days, while their emotions are still fresh and they know little theology, their testimonies have a vibrancy but also a rawness. They tell as much as they know. Later, after they've been absorbed into the life of the church, their testimonies become more theologically sound and knowledgeable. Are they lying later on? I don't think so. Without conscious awareness, growth in their theological understanding since conversion influences the way they relate their memories.

Here's another nonsexual illustration of what I mean. I drove a Dodge from our then-home in northern Illinois to upstate New York. I pulled a trailer with the things we planned to ship to Kenya. In northern Ohio, I couldn't make it up a steep incline and pulled over onto the shoulder. I planned to unhook the trailer, turn the car around, and go back down. Before I could do that, a Cadillac tried to pass a Chevrolet going up the hill just as a Ford came down. There was a three-way crash. No one was hurt in the accident, but the impact forced the Ford over to the shoulder, and it hit the left front side of our Dodge. We were outside the car and were almost struck by the Ford. That much Shirley and I agreed on.

Perhaps ten years later, I told the story and Shirley said, "No, it wasn't quite like that." She told details that seemed wrong to me. We didn't argue about it, but I assumed she had forgotten the real story. Less than a year after that, Shirley's mother died. In her belongings we found all the letters I'd written from Africa. In the first one, which I'd written just hours after the accident, I went into detail. Shirley and I remembered things differently, and both of us were wrong about the details.

That's normal. That's human. Because of that, when my memories began to return, I suspected every one. Even today, I don't know how many are absolutely factual. I do know many are accurate, or at least close enough so that I have no question that the assaults were real.

Two things convinced me of the reality of some or all of my "memories." First, I had verification from my siblings, especially from two of my sisters. Second, I still have a few issues, such as my inability to eat raspberry jam. I know the male perpetrator fed it to me on soda crackers. I've dealt with many things, but even today I still become nauseated if I try to eat raspberry jam. Even though I know the reason, my intense dislike of raspberry jam hasn't disappeared.

I have other memories, some vague and others quite clear. I don't know if they're retrievals of actual experiences or something I've unconsciously concocted from an active imagination. Enough of them have been verified that I know I was molested, and I know both of the perpetrators. That's what's most important. The questionable memories I can leave behind.

Today there is controversy, however, over what have been called *false memories, pseudomemories,* and *memory illusions.* These are imaginings that one sincerely believes are true but are not based in historical reality. They can result from the influence of external factors, such as the opinion of an authority figure or information repeated in one's culture. An individual with an internal desire to please, to get better, or to conform can easily be affected by such influences.

What Is the Recovered-Memory Controversy About?

In cases of sexual molestation, skeptics are concerned that memories often occur years after the alleged events. And the victims can offer no external corroboration. It's not a question of if the abuse has taken place, or a claim that people can't remember severe childhood trauma. But there are many reasons why people don't remember something: childhood amnesia, physical trauma, drugs, or even the natural decay of stored information. Thus, the controversy revolves around the accuracy of those recovered memories of sexual assault.

What If He Thinks He "Might Have Been" Abused?

Is it possible to suffer such childhood abuse that a man forgets permanently? Or is it that he has buried the memories so deeply within his subconscious mind that he can't get in touch with them? How could he have experienced something so traumatic and not remember?

Not to remember is one survival technique of adults who were abused in childhood. Our minds protect us from what we can't accept. I don't know the answer to those who think they might have been molested but have no focused recollection. Throughout the rest of this book, though, I write about not only the memories but the effects. It's possible to retrieve some memories by beginning with some of the results or unexplainable behavior. For many of us, the journey to healing starts even though we don't have immediate access to the events through our recollections. For others, memory retrieval begins with a feeling that something dreadful and fearful happened. That fear may paralyze us for a long time before we figure out what took place.

One friend said, "I had the sense that something bad happened, but for a couple of years it was as if the memory hid around the next corner, and I couldn't catch it." He also said, "Once I was ready to face the unfaceable, memories began to trickle into my consciousness." He said that it helped him understand why he avoided one family member.

One survivor freaked out when he saw a curly-haired man at the beach wearing a string bikini. I have an olfactory memory: the smell of a certain kind of talcum powder that my female perpetrator used is still vivid to me. Before I dealt with my abuse, that smell bothered me. Other talcum fragrances were fine, but that one made me feel as if my sinuses were clogged. Sometimes when a woman came near me wearing the same brand, I wanted to run out of the building.

The controversy has arisen, however, especially during the last decade, that when those with vague feelings or unclear memories speak with some professionals, some of those clients are harmed. Instead of receiving help or treatment, they accept nudges and suggestions by the professionals. I find it incredulous that a professional would intentionally induce false memories; I do find it credible, however, that some professionals "see" abuse when there may not have been any. I knew a psychiatric nurse, for instance, who'd been the victim of incest. She once told me, "I can spot abused people—male or female—as soon as they walk into the room."

Maybe she was right. But what if she was wrong? What if she worked with a man and suggested that he might have been sexually assaulted? What if that man was highly susceptible? What if he accepted those suggestions as truth but he hadn't been molested? What if he conjured up memories that weren't real? It happens.

I'll always be grateful to my friend—who is also a therapist—David Morgan. Although he suspected my abuse, he didn't do anything to suggest or to lead me in that direction. He loved me, and his caring helped me to open wide the door to my healing. That's the difference. I was the one who first said the word *molested*.

*   *   *

The question becomes whether recollections of abuse are repressed memories or false memories. That's still a hot issue among the professionals, and I'm hardly qualified to give definite answers. I do have a few thoughts, however. We know that if a boy is severely stressed by a traumatic event, it affects his brain chemistry. Trauma acts like a medication that takes away pain and results in not only repression, denial, and dissociation (a serious psychological issue that is beyond the scope of this book) but the loss of memory as well. It's not surprising that as the boy matures he would "forget" what happened to him in an effort to survive or to protect himself from the psychic pain.

Later, however, those memories resurface, often spontaneously. We who were abused face grim realities. The fact that we survived at all is a testimony of our inner strength and more so a testimony of God's loving grace. Having to cope with a lot more than most children do, we sometimes took our survival for granted. Not all of us, though, cope enough to survive. Some children and teens take their own lives.

"It hurt too much," my friend Monroe who'd attempted suicide told me. "I didn't want to die but I couldn't live with the pain." After he shot himself in the stomach and recovered, his boss told him that he had to see some kind of counselor if he wanted to come back to work. He did. "That's when I admitted the sexual abuse and faced the real pain," he said.

Once Monroe opened the door, the memories flooded back. He went into voluntary psychiatric lockup for thirty days so he could get daily help. "The staff there saved my life," he said. As much as any survivor might want to remember details, Monroe's mind, until that attempted suicide, continued to protect him and refused to let him remember.

Monroe isn't that unusual. The adult survivor generally wants to forget the hurt of the past. It's not easy to move beyond the pain, but it is possible. Healing rarely comes instantaneously, but each day he can move farther down the road of recovery.

9

IF HIS ABUSER WAS A WOMAN

For many years it was unthinkable that a woman would molest a boy. But it was probably almost as unthinkable that a priest or a church elder could be a pedophile. Such realities no longer shock us—or at least not as they did in the 1990s when the first stories came out.

When the perpetrator is a woman, the effects of the abuse on the victim often are more acute. It's difficult enough for a boy to understand what is happening when a male touches him inappropriately or forces himself on the boy. But it's far worse for the victim to face the reality that his sister or aunt involved him in sexual acts. When the abuser is the mother, the situation seems even more horrendous.

Mother-son incest (which is the correct term) is the most taboo of all human relationships, and it's condemned by every culture. When I've brought the subject up in lectures, I've received blank stares of unbelief or horror. One time a woman cried out, "No mother could do that."

"They can. They do." I've answered. I've known a handful of men who know what mothers can do.

The point I want to make is that mother-son incest is horrendous and next to impossible for many people to believe. We're so caught up in the idea of mothers being Madonna-like figures that it's difficult to comprehend how some women could do such things to their own sons. *But they do.*

"I sat in class in eighth grade when our teacher read us some poem about a mother who willingly gave her life for her son," said Boyd. "I think she donated a kidney." Tears ran down his face when he related the incident to our state-sponsored group. It took Boyd several minutes before he was able to talk. That night was the first time we had mentioned women who sexually assault boys.

"Let me tell you the rest of this," Boyd said. "When the teacher finished reading, she said, 'Mother love is the most unselfish love in the world.' The teacher went on to expound on the topic.

"I put my head on my desk and cried. The teacher misunderstood my reaction and said to the class, 'See. Here's someone who understands that poem.'"

Boyd told us, "Oh, I understood all right! I understood a monster possessed my mother!"

Any abuse affects a boy, but this might be the worst form, because the mother-son relationship is the most sacred of human relationships. Men who were sexually abused by their mothers, or other women in parenting roles, such as sisters, aunts, or grandmothers, often feel inner turmoil, shame, guilt, and self-loathing. That's not merely my opinion. Therapists, including my friend David Morgan, seem to agree.

These boys were betrayed by the women who were supposed to take care of them and to protect them. Abuse by a mother is often the last to be dealt with when there have been other perpetrators in the survivor's history. Many men say that the abuse by their mothers was the most shameful and damaging form of childhood victimization they experienced.

Those whose mothers sexually molested them often have difficulty in disclosing the abuse because they feel a strange sense of loyalty to their mothers. Someone called it a *trauma bond*—it's conflicted and troublesome, but still a bond. That loyalty may stop the abused from opening up.

"Even though my head knew," one man said, "in my heart, I felt I would be betraying my mother's trust." He laughed self-consciously before he said, "It doesn't make sense when I talk about it, but my feelings and my head haven't always worked together."

In the yearlong state-sponsored group in which I was involved, one of the therapists pointed out that in such relationships, the son often takes on the role of the husband.

Boyd perked up over those words. "My mother started fondling me and things like that when I was small, maybe five or six years old. Maybe earlier, I don't remember. It got worse as I got older. She'd bring me into her bed after Dad went to work. 'Let's cuddle,' she'd say. And that's how the abuse started; and it got worse."

He said it continued until he was thirteen. "I refused to get into bed with her after that. I made up excuses about homework or needing to get to school early, but I didn't give in."

Boyd told us about the home dynamics. Whenever his parents argued, he was always on his mother's side—even when he knew she was wrong. "It didn't seem right not to stand with her." He wanted to please her and felt he "had to take care of her."

A close friend was sexually abused by his mother, and I know the effects it had on him. He grew up taking care of his mother. Whenever problems arose, she went to him to solve them. He moved more than a thousand miles away from home to go to college, but she called him regularly, soliciting his advice. He had two older sisters, who lived nearby, but she wanted only his advice. Even though she had a husband, she relied on her son—whom she had molested in childhood.

That son became a submissive adult and was extremely kind and caring to women. His wife mentioned that he cared for the house better than she did. Other men go the opposite way. For them, *all* women are manipulators and controlling. Gary, for example, a pastor-friend who has since died, told me about his mother's abuse. He hated women, although he was married three times. I met him between his second and third marriage and knew his third wife. She was a kind, caring person, but he was abusive even during the courtship. He yelled at her in public, and when he and I were alone, he insisted she was running around. (I'm convinced he was totally wrong.) When his wife finally became pregnant, Gary told me, "That's all she wants from me anyway. I'm just a stud to provide a kid."

I didn't understand him for a long time—and we became friends just about the time I began to deal with my own abuse. Only in retrospect did I grasp how deeply his childhood trauma had affected him.

Some of the forms of abuse by a mother—or by any female—can be disguised, or accomplished through manipulation. One man told us that his mother used to get in the tub and ask him to help her bathe. He was an adolescent before he finally was able to stop washing her back and her breasts.

It is common for women who sexually assault their sons to use emotional manipulation and control. A mother tells her son, for example, that doing a certain act will make mommy "feel good." For his compliance the child receives kisses and hugs, and she pretends that the abuse is really a form of washing her body. And what child wouldn't want to please his mother?

One man challenged his mother at age twelve about what was going on and she laughed at him. "It's because we share such a loving relationship that we do this." She went on to say, "I love you, and no woman will ever, ever love you as deeply as I do." Even though that man is married to a good woman, he still struggles with that manipulative behavior from his childhood.

Although it's not often reported, mothers and other female perpetrators can be violent. This is particularly evident in ritual abuse during which women, along with men, are sadistic toward children (and adults). These cases have been exposed, yet the stereotype and reality of the "emotionally clingy" female perpetrator is given more attention because it confirms our beliefs that women are weak, emotionally dependent, and nonviolent. But I've heard horrendous stories from men (and from women) who were beaten and tortured by their mothers, and not only in the context of ritual abuse.

Until quite recently, books, articles, and Web sites didn't refer to women molesting boys. Because it's been ignored through silence, many male survivors live in isolation, fear, shame, and anger. They can't talk about it or don't know how to talk about it.

For some men, it's difficult even to admit that their mothers were the abusers. Twice in conducting retreats for men, I've mentioned mothers as perpetrators and received horrified responses from the men. We know it happens but the cultural myths continue to insist that mothers love their sons unselfishly; mothers always have their children's best interests at heart; mothers are always there to meet the needs of their offspring; mothers are never sexually attracted to their sons; even if she were attracted to boys, she wouldn't molest her child.

The first person I heard mention mother-son abuse was a writer named Marty. He joined our writers' group and was quite active. He and I became good friends. One night we sat on my front steps in the dark and he said, "I want to tell you something I've told only one other person."

His words shocked me. When Marty was fifteen, he came home one night and his single-parent mother was drunk and had passed out on the sofa. He tried to get her off the couch and help her walk upstairs to bed. She began to kiss him, fondle him, and take off his clothes.

The next morning, he didn't know what to say, and she never brought it up. A few months later she tried it again, but he pushed her back on the sofa and walked away.

All mother-son incest isn't so obvious. Sometimes it masquerades as some aspect of loving care such as hygiene—a mother may refuse to allow her son to wash his own genitals. It might be as simple as holding him too tightly and pressing her body into his.

Regardless of the responses of an uninformed culture, the reality is that boys *are* sexually abused by women. Some people view it as impossible because they insist a male can't be sexually assaulted by a female. Others view it as sexually titillating.

The existence of female perpetrators and male victims challenges many of our most firmly held beliefs about women, men, sexuality, power, and sexual assault. It challenges, in fact, our very notions about what sex is.

— *10* —

THE EFFECTS OF ABUSE

Every man is an individual; every abuse survivor will have different symptoms. You'll read that statement several times in this book because that's an important thing to remember. No one can lay down ten principles for recovery and no one can promise healing. Here are a few questions, however, that—whether or not he has told you any of his story— might help you understand the particular situation of the man you care about.

Did He Tell Anyone?

If he remained silent in childhood, the symptoms may stay hidden or masked for years. Those of us who remained silent pushed the pain deeper inside.

When I was being abused I never told anyone, and I have no awareness of the reason I withheld the information. As I look back, I think it was because of shame and guilt. My mother was an expert at inducing both emotions. I grew up saying that I ate three generous helpings of guilt every day. I've come to believe that with our limited childish wisdom we have a sense about when it's safe to tell and when it's not.

If He Did Tell, What Was the Response?

Responses of ignoring, blaming, and shaming damage those already vulnerable children. Such negative responses can cause as much harm as the assault itself. Another response is disbelief—or the child may have assumed no one believed him.

In chapter 1, I mentioned the meeting of seven of us at Oglethorpe University. One of the men said his father abused him, and he knew it was wrong. When he was ten, he told us, the torment had built up until he decided he had to do something. The family sat at the table one evening and no one said a word, which was typical of their family. Previously, he'd tried to work up the courage to say something, but he always held back. That night the pressure became so heavy, he blurted out, "Dad's been molesting me and I want it to stop."

His mother looked up at him and said, "Pass the gravy. I don't want my potatoes to get cold."

No one said another word. No one looked at anyone else.

The abuse didn't stop until he was almost fourteen. "It stopped because I was big enough to stand up to him." He had grown taller and broader than his father. One night his father came into his room late at night. The boy was propped up in bed and held a baseball bat. "If you touch me again, I'll beat you with this bat, even if I have to kill you."

He admitted to us that his words were exaggerated, but he said, "I couldn't take it again."

His father never came back into his room late at night.

It's remarkable to what extent the sexual abuse of boys continues to be denied in families, especially if one of the family members is the perpetrator. In a lecture, one man said something like this: "The politics of silence is a perfect accomplice to those who abuse boys."

I've listened to horrible descriptions of childhood assault. One man said it was like a mouse being repeatedly caught in a trap. "I wasn't drawn to the cheese. The trap chased me and constantly caught me."

It's not surprising that many men who were abused in childhood turn to alcohol, drugs, or even suicide. I'm convinced that my two younger brothers who medicated their pain with alcohol were never able to talk about their abuse, and died from the results.

When the abuse is father-son incest, the boy's world is turned upside down. It results in a loss of the identity references a normal family provides. The incest leaves the boy questioning what he ought to be able to take for granted. "Am I a man?" is a common question—one he shouldn't have to ask himself. "Am I normal? Who is my father? Is he my father or my lover? Is he my friend or my enemy? Does he love me? Am I supposed to obey him and become like him? Why doesn't Mom protect me?"

Father-son abuse is the double taboo of incest and homosexuality. The men who've talked to me usually said they endured because, for a long time, they didn't realize it wasn't normal. They didn't talk about it or ask questions. Each one didn't have much of a relationship with his male parent before the abuse began. As distasteful as it was, the abuse offered these boys attention and affection. Most of them hoped that it would lead to a better relationship. It didn't.

A few men have said that it was such a constant occurrence they assumed all boys went through the same thing. They didn't talk about it because they assumed all adults wanted to have sex with children.

What Support Was Available?

Did he have supportive family members or someone in whom he could confide? Were negative feelings acceptable in the home? How much did he internalize and blame himself for the assault?

My observation is that most of the abused men I met were driven by an intense quest for affection or love. They often perceived both parents—not just the father—as indifferent, distant, or rejecting them. In my case, I truly didn't feel accepted or wanted in my childhood.

Of every molested male with whom I've talked, none of them mentioned violence or rape. Violence happened later when one of them wanted to break off the "relationship." But in the beginning, the molesters showed interest in us. The perpetrators were kind to us and made us feel accepted. Many of us accepted the abuse in silence because we felt accepted or attached to the older persons who exploited our affection for their own compulsions. We were so desperate that we would have done almost anything to feel loved. That need made us easy prey to pedophiles.

It seems to make a significant difference if an abused boy had a childhood confidant such as an older boy, a friend, or a pastor. Research indicates that if abused boys have someone in whom they can confide—someone they can trust—even if they don't talk about their abuse, they tend to grow up with fewer problems than boys who felt forced to keep secrets.

Why didn't I speak up? Why didn't I tell someone, even a school friend? I've asked myself that hundreds of times. I've come up with only one possibility: *I didn't think anyone cared.* Who was there to support me or to comfort me? Whether accurate or not, those were my feelings. As a child, my feelings *were* my reality. I had no close friends in childhood or anyone in whom I felt I could confide.

The female relative who abused my two younger brothers and me wasn't someone I could have accused. It happened when we were so young, how did we know it was abuse? I don't want to go into details but it included her fondling us and forcing us to do the same to her. Even after I was in my early teens, that female relative used to tell me explicitly sexual jokes. When I was as old as fifteen, she embraced me with her whole body—and I detested myself for evil thoughts. Perhaps that's one reason some of us didn't talk: we assumed something was wrong with us.

Those who should have been the best confidants, such as relatives, Sunday school teachers, pastors, and guidance counselors, have often been the abusers. They are authority figures, individuals we trusted, those who should have encouraged us and taken care of us.

There is power in admitting to and describing traumatic experiences. Molested males need to find ways to express what happened. Being able to articulate their experiences through speaking about it, writing about it, journaling, or some other form often provides a powerful tool for overcoming their pain because the process itself helps to make sense out of their experiences. As they do so, they progress toward mental health.

How Long Did the Assault Continue?

Was it a one-time event or something that continued? Even one experience can traumatize individuals. Repeated abuse compounds the pain. Stanley, for instance, was repeatedly molested when he was in foster care. "From the front window, I watched every afternoon as [my abuser] came up the walk. I could tell by the way he walked if he would come after me that night."

Stanley was only six, but he had developed the vigilance to detect the signs that warned him that one of the boys in the house would be molested that night. Three boys lived there at the time, so Stanley learned to figure out ways not to be the one chosen.

"When I sensed he was going to go after one of us, I'd stay away from him until dinner. As soon as dinner was over and I'd dried dishes—which was my evening chore—I hid from him. On the nights he decided he wanted me, he searched until he found me. He tried to make a big joke out of searching for me. When we were alone, he molested me and sometimes beat me for hiding from him. He said he only wanted to love me."

Boys like Stanley often have more severe problems because of the duration of the abuse. I met Stanley in 1990, and he had been in recovery four years. At our last connection around 1997, he said, "I'm better, but I still struggle."

What Does He Do Now to Cope?

He can't change what happened to him during childhood. He was sexually molested. It will always be part of his life story. But it's possible for him to stop the self-destructive, self-defeating things he does to himself as well as the hurtful things he does to others because of his painful past.

Recovery and healing isn't easy. He probably won't remember all the facts, and it might be difficult for him to face the world realistically, to sort out what matters, what's threatening, what people truly mean when they compliment him or get angry at him.

The more open he is to talk about the sexual assault, the easier it will be for him to heal. First, though, he needs to know that he doesn't have to be afraid of how the significant people—or person—in his life will respond. He needs to accept that God loves him and has promised to give him the strength he needs. The person in his life who most embodies compassion and understanding is quite often a loving woman. The more that woman shows him those qualities, the more she can point him to a loving, caring God.

11

THE INNER ABUSER

For healing to take place, the man who was abused needs to come to terms with how the abuse affects his attitudes and behavior toward himself and toward others. As a child he received strong messages about his worth. A man I remember only as Dale said his older brother sodomized him and afterward would say, "You're only good for one thing."

"For a long time I believed him," Dale said. When he was in college, Dale met a campus minister who befriended him. "He taught me that I wasn't useless except for sex." That was the first step in Dale's seven-year struggle to recover.

The Effect of Words

Some messages are delivered and take hold in a more subtle way. The words Dale and others heard aren't as important as how the words affected them. At some time, someone may have joked or made a careless remark, but if the hearer accepts the remark as true, the words change him.

Suppose a father says to his son, even in joking, "You're a wimp." Those words can take permanent root. I see it this way: if those words, no matter how lightly spoken, touched the uncertain areas of a boy's life, he tends to believe them. He may not be a wimp, but if he has reservations or concerns about his masculinity—and most boys do—those words would stick. Or a mother might say, "You're ugly." She may or may not mean that, but those words linger in a boy's psyche.

Again, I'll illustrate from my own life. My father was forty years old when I was born, and I had four older siblings. It almost seems like they had a different father than I did. When I was still a preschooler, Dad expected me to do chores that were demanding for kids my age. When I performed satisfactorily, he was silent; when I failed, he called me a "lazy wart." I never understood the *wart* part but I grasped the message. I believed him: I thought I was lazy. I spent most of my teen and adult years trying to prove to Dad that I wasn't lazy. I'm sure (now) that he didn't think so, but I had absorbed those words that he spoke, probably in one of his many fits of anger.

Abused boys, already traumatized, often carry those negative messages inside their heads. The words exert a powerful influence. Even when those boys become adults, the messages remain so ingrained the victims don't even question them.

Those messages become what I call *the inner abuser*. The inner abuser is the voice that calls the adult survivor incompetent, fat, ugly, or stupid. The inner abuser criticizes him at every opportunity. The words—and often the accompanying emotions—remain, and that accusing voice undermines his best efforts and attacks in many ways. It will continue to intrude unless he gets rid of them. Getting rid of them isn't easy, but it can be done.

Cary's father not only sexually assaulted his son but told him he was worthless and that he'd never amount to anything. Cary believed him. His one accomplishment was that he graduated from college—barely. But the voice inside his head said, "But if you were worth anything you would have been on the dean's list."

I knew Cary for several years, and he was one of those people who, as they say, shot himself in the foot. He would get close to a promising job or career step, then just before it happened, he did something stupid or said the wrong thing. He failed, was passed over for promotion, or even was fired from two good jobs. Every time he failed the voice whispered, "See, you'll always fail."

Even though his IQ scores and aptitude tests showed him in the high percentile, Cary remained a junior-grade accountant in a large banking firm. At one point he trained people who became his supervisors.

Did he ever get past all that? I don't know. He joined a small group of male survivors during a four-year period when we lived in Louisville, Kentucky. He faced his sexual and verbal abuse, working with a therapist who specialized in sexual issues. The last time I saw Cary, he'd decided to quit his job and move to Washington, D.C. "I want to start over," he said.

I hope that's what he did.

✦ ✦ ✦

The inner abuser shows up in relationships. He might be too willing to take the blame for everything that goes wrong. Or he may refuse to take any blame. He may argue over things that seem entirely insignificant or he may never disagree with anyone.

Those inner-abuse messages, repeatedly spoken to a boy, inevitably result in a sense of low self-worth. Either he tends to become what that inner-abuse voice says or he rebels and fights it constantly. Without understanding what that voice is and where it originates, it's difficult for him to keep up the battle.

Our sense of self-worth is made up of personal beliefs and messages that reflect how we value ourselves. As children, much of our self-esteem or self-worth came from the significant adults in our lives, usually our parents, but maybe adult relatives and teachers were significant too. When an abuser is also a significant person, the child victim incorporated subtle or negative messages that accompanied his abuse.

Self-worth is a serious issue with all adult survivors. The abuse left them with feelings of shame, helplessness, or perhaps a sense of incompetence. Because they internalized those words, the words play repeatedly inside their heads. The endless playback of the inner-abuse messages leads them to actions that further lower their sense of self-worth. The words are probably so ingrained the survivors are not aware of them.

I mentioned earlier that my father called me lazy. I didn't think about his words, but my actions reflected that I had absorbed the abusive words. Today people remark on my high level of energy, which is accurate. What they don't know, and I didn't grasp until I was in my forties, is that I couldn't admit to being tired. If I said I was tired that showed everyone I was lazy.

My behavior was strange as I look back at it but to show the absurdity of my situation, I'll give you another example. My dad called me lazy on several occasions. My *unconscious* goal was to prove him wrong. At one time I went full-time to two graduate schools and graduated second in my class at one of them. Why wasn't I first? If I hadn't been lazy I could have worked harder and been number one. That's nonsense, and what difference did it make? In the years since, no one ever asked me about my position in the graduating class. I know it's not important—*I know it now*—but in those days, to work harder was a compulsion over which I seemed to have no control. The inner abuser was at work inside my head.

I think inner abuse is sexual abuse the second time around. An adult survivor may feel the same way he did as a child victim because he may continue to victimize himself. He can't be free until *he* knows the false messages are lies. As long as he believes them, he's still being victimized and inwardly abused.

Once I began to deal with my abuse, I became aware that those self-abuse messages weren't true. I wasn't lazy and I wasn't bad. Before I became aware of the abuse, I was even critical and judgmental of other people. I wasn't aware of it, but I criticized myself most of all.

I received help during the year I was a member of a state-sponsored group of male survivors. One of the therapists said, "Those are mental tapes, and they don't belong to you. They were lies told to you. You kept them stored inside and played them regularly, but they're not yours. You listen to them faithfully every day, but you don't have to do that." He went on to say that those self-abuse tapes try to keep us from progressing and succeeding, and we're abused all over again.

With me, and with most abuse victims, most of our negative self-talk messages were recorded in our brains years ago. They represent a part of the abuser that had been incorporated into our psyches. After I became aware of those messages and that they were lies, I determined to eradicate them. I read a couple of books about the importance of self-talk, and I began to incorporate the principles.

As I mention elsewhere, I run early in the mornings, and it's a special time of prayer for me. That's where my change began and much of my healing took place. On 3x5 file cards, I wrote simple, positive, hoped-to-realize statements for myself. As I ran I repeated them to myself. For the first few weeks, I read each one ten times. There's no magic in the number, only that they were so difficult to say aloud, I had to say them repeatedly.

After a few weeks, I said them fewer times each day. I kept up that practice for at least two years. For me, it was the way to evict those self-abuse messages and allow self-affirming ones to take up residence. I asked the Lord to help me embrace the new messages. I don't know how much the gurus of self-talk really know, but they said to phrase everything in the positive and in the present. Instead of saying, "I am not lazy," I said, "I am energetic."

Here are a few other positive statements I repeated to myself:

+ "I am lovable because God created me lovable."
+ "I am worthwhile because God made me worthwhile."
+ "I am good because God enables me to be good."

I incorporated God into each positive, self-talk statement. My self-talk wasn't some kind of secular, help-yourself, pop psychology. It was my cry to God to enable me to accept the truths I spoke and for me to realize that everything I am and everything I have are divine gifts from a loving God.

I no longer need my new messages. The new ones destroyed the power of those negative, inner-abuse messages. But that wasn't enough for me. I wanted to make my commitment to healing even stronger. For a period of at least a year, I copied Bible verses on cards and memorized them as I ran in the dark. It was something I hadn't done for years. In my early Christian days I learned the Navigator's Topical Memory System. One of the first verses I learned in the King James Version was Psalm 119:11: "Thy word have I hid in mine heart, that I might not sin against thee."

Many of those verses strengthened my commitment to see myself as a lovable, honorable, and worthwhile human being. In taking those steps—and they worked for me—I realized that the inner abuser is most powerful when we don't recognize its presence.

✦   ✦   ✦

The adult survivor needs to come face-to-face with the inner voices that have guided much of his life. If he does, he can begin to become aware of how he's been affected and why he has done certain things. The more conscious he becomes of those secret tapes, the less power the inner abuser has over him.

He can overcome the inner abuser. He can win. An important thing he can do is say to himself that he is worthwhile. He can ask God to help him believe that he was not responsible for the abuse. He is, however, responsible for how he deals with its effects. As an adult he needs to accept the reality that he has a problem with his attitude and behavior, and with God's help, he can change. It can be powerful for him to say simple statements about himself every day:

- ✦ "I can do all things through Christ who strengthens me."
- ✦ "I push away the old, painful messages and embrace the truth."
- ✦ "I am learning to love myself. I can do that because God loves me."

The Lies He Might Believe

Because someone stole his childhood, the adult survivor may have believed or bought into lies. Here are the obvious ones.

It was my fault.

Even if he acknowledges that he was assaulted, he may feel it was partially his fault.

"I didn't make him stop."

"I didn't run away."

"I didn't tell anyone."

"I liked it, so something must be wrong with me."

That's all nonsense, of course. It wasn't his fault and he didn't do anything wrong. How could he run away or fight if the perpetrator was a family member or someone he encountered regularly? Research indicates that most instances of sexual abuse aren't perpetrated by some man who roams the streets after dark. It's someone the victim knows—someone he ought to be able to trust.

The adult survivor, though, loses sight of the fact that he was an innocent child at the time and instead imagines what he might have done as an adult.

It was a terrible thing he did, but he really loved me.

Perpetrators are con artists. They know the words to say that their victims yearn to hear. They prey on children who are lonely, who feel unloved, or who need attention and affection.

Pedophiles will say or do anything to manipulate and control a victim. The abuser may have said "I'm doing this because I love you." The adult survivor, again, may lose sight of the fact that as a victim he was an object of anything but love. Instead of receiving love, the child was taken advantage of, hurt, and betrayed.

God will deal with him. I need to leave it in God's hands.

That sounds spiritual, but it's an evasion. It's also true that, ultimately, the abuser will have to face God for what he did. For the victim to face his past isn't about revenge or making the perpetrator pay for his sin. It's about healing. Only as the molested survivor copes with the issue will there be resolution.

He probably went through a long period when he kept silent about the abuse. He did nothing. He no longer needs to keep silent and push away the painful memories. Until he can bring his feelings to the surface and admit them, he's still being victimized. He's still living in silence. As long as he remains the victim, he can't go forward with his spiritual and mental growth.

Think of the abuse as a fallen tree that blocks the highway. He can't go around it. He can deny that he needs to go anywhere and can turn around and go back home. Or he can do the most sensible thing: he can remove the tree. If it's too big to move by himself, he can call for others to help him.

It wasn't that bad.

He may tell himself that the abuse could have lasted longer or been more frequent. Or the abuse might not have been as severe with him as it was with other children. "He only made me . . ."

The extent or duration isn't the point. No matter what the perpetrator did, it was wrong. It was sin. It damaged that child. For the adult survivor to minimize the trauma or the damage is a form of denial. It's a lie to himself that enables him to feel less guilty or dirty, but it only gets in the way of his healing.

To say, "It wasn't that bad," keeps the lie going and hinders his recovery.

Of course it could have been worse. The perpetrator could have maimed him. He could have killed him. Does the "could have beens" make the abuse better? Does it lessen the pain just to know that he's alive?

If he wants healing, he needs to be open about the abuse. *It was bad. It was terrible.* That's what he needs to face.

Something must be wrong with me. I mean, it felt good.

That's one of the problems sexually abused boys have to face. That the penis becomes stimulated is a natural phenomenon. That's the way God made male bodies. Certain kinds of touch feel good and may have aroused him sexually. That's simple biology.

One of the abominable tricks of perpetrators is that they say, "That feels good, doesn't it?" If it feels good, to a child's mind it must *be* good. At the same time, though (or later), he might ask himself, "If it was good, why do I feel guilty?"

Abusers know touch gives the child pleasurable, sexual feelings, but it's not for the benefit of the child. Pedophiles have only one concern: their own sexual enjoyment. That it felt good to the child only made it easier for the perpetrator to take advantage of him.

There wasn't anything wrong with the child; there was something terribly, terribly wrong with the adult. The victim needs to remember that.

✦   ✦   ✦

Besides the loss of innocence, the survivor suffered a breach of physical integrity—someone violated his body by inducement or force. The pedophile exposed that child to disease and to psychic wounds related to abusive sexual activity. If that's not true, why is the adult survivor suffering now? Why are there psychological scars and deep inner pain? Why does he have low self-esteem and feelings of low self-worth?

Child sexual abuse is quite possibly the worst kind of betrayal. The abuser lied to the victim or tricked him or took advantage of an established relationship. He was likely a relative, a neighbor, or a friend of the family. As the adult, that person was supposed to have cared for the boy and protected him. As the adult, he wasn't supposed to hurt or damage the boy, but he did. The adult refused to stop when the boy pleaded with him. He ignored the child's cry for help. How, then, can that fit any of the lies of the inner abuser? How can that be love? How can such behavior be excused because it felt good? When the abuser is a person to whom the boy has been entrusted, the only word I come up with is *betrayal*.

Another dynamic of inner abuse is that because the betrayal was by someone trusted—or someone a child expected could be trusted—it made the boy feel powerless. The child couldn't stop the violation of his body. He was small and young; the perpetrator was older and stronger. If the adult survivor is typical, he judges himself harshly for what he perceives as weaknesses. He felt powerless to get help; he felt powerless to talk about it. I understand that sense of powerlessness.

I know that I suffered as an adult and accused myself harshly. My victimization increased because of that powerlessness. How could it be otherwise? When boys like me feel alone, ignored, or unloved, we have no place to flee. We don't trust anyone enough to tell, and we think we're disgusting to other people. We endured or we began self-destructive acts. As I've previously mentioned, many of those who have been abused become susceptible to alcohol or drugs or even compulsive sexual activity as ways to ease their pain. Those things work—for a short time—but they don't cure anything.

Another contributor to inner abuse is a word I'd never heard until long after my recovery—"stigmatization." It refers to feelings of shame, guilt, disgrace, isolation, and especially self-blame. Such feelings victims intuitively pick up from our environment—the family, church, neighborhood, school—and tie in with our negative self-image. Not only were we victimized by a powerful, older person, but we're victimized a second time by our emotional responses.

When I was in ninth grade, our male English teacher often sat on the edge of a desk, his legs apart. His fly was partially open, and no one dared to say anything. About the second month of school and with no explanation we got a new English teacher. Within a day or two after the new teacher arrived, the rumors flew—and they were probably true. The former teacher had sexually abused one boy named Carl (or at least that's the name I remember). Carl told on him and the teacher was gone.

The sad thing was that the kids avoided Carl. They made crude jokes about him and sometimes made fun of him. They called him names behind his back, although I'm sure Carl was aware.

I wasn't able to deal with my own abuse—I'd developed amnesia long before that—but I felt sorry for him. I didn't do anything to hurt him and don't recall that I did anything to help. And yet I remember that incident clearly. I witnessed the stigma that Carl endured. He was ostracized because he was the victim who told.

I don't know what happened to Carl. I know only that he didn't go into high school with the rest of us. I've thought about him many times over the past few years. Each time I think, *That poor kid. He was victimized twice.*

In fact, he may have been victimized three times. Not only the abuse itself and the unkind attitude from the other boys, but from the inner abuse that resulted from the damage done to Carl's psyche.

I wonder how many Carls there are.

12

TYPICAL SYMPTOMS

"Do you understand what I mean? Does that make sense?"

At first thought, you might think those questions sound innocuous—and often they are. But when the adult survivor asks, the questions may have far more significance. What is he *really* asking? He might be seeking more than confirmation that you've understood what he's just said. It might be a plea for help.

Sometimes he may ask, "Don't you think that . . . ?" That might be his way of pleading, "Please tell me that I'm right. Tell me I'm not wrong."

He may not even be aware of the intent of his words, but his words should be taken with utter seriousness. It's as if he's saying, "I'm trying to make sense of my world. The things I've just said to you, are they correct or am I crazy?" He might be pleading, "Please tell me that I'm not crazy." Sometimes his tormenting thoughts may make him question what's real and what's imaginary.

Confusion and Control

The world of childhood sexual assault has left the victim confused. He was deceived and lied to as a child. Why wouldn't such significant events have an impact on his understanding of life?

"When they passed out the book of life's rules," one man said, "I didn't get a copy. I had to peek over the shoulders of others and missed many of the significant lessons."

He may see others as more self-assured and happy than he. They seem secure and have their world figured out. He wishes he had that kind of self-confidence. He may try to make it seem as if he does by bragging or exaggerating, but it's often a cover-up.

When he asks a question, then, sometimes it's not the *real* question. That is, there's *a question behind the question*.

Ken, as an example unrelated to sexual abuse, was a new writer. He asked, "Is there any money in this business?" Although a simple question, that wasn't what he wanted to know. He meant, "Can I make a living at writing?" He asked it in a general way, but the question was specifically about himself.

When I answered, I did so as if he'd asked the underlying question. I explained how hard *he* would have to work to make money as a writer. He didn't become a writer, by the way.

I remember Bernard in our state-sponsored group because of the precision of his language. I don't think I've ever heard anyone who carefully enunciated every word as clearly as he did. One time I mispronounced a word and he corrected me—in a scolding manner. He did that to others as well.

After the members of our group got to know him better, Tommy challenged, "You need to correct everyone, don't you?"

"That's just the way I am," Bernard said.

"No, that's the way you've become," Tommy said.

We sat through a lengthy silence, and it was obvious Bernard was thinking deeply. I didn't know if he was trying to figure it out or if he already knew and struggled with whether to tell us.

He slowly explained that it was his way to be accepted as an authority on the language. To be correct made him feel worthwhile. The following week he thanked us for intervening and said, "I convinced myself that if I had been able to speak up and say no, my stepfather wouldn't have abused me."

He blamed himself for his confusion as a child and his lack of ability to be more articulate. It may sound strange that his inability as a child to articulate showed itself as a precision in adult language skills. But that's how the effects of abuse work; they come out in our behavior, but rarely in a straight line. That's one reason it's difficult for those of us with amnesia to face the reality and results of our abuse.

I understood Bernard, and I realized his need for precision in expressing language was close to one of my own defenses. As a child, when I entered a room in which either of my abusers was present, I had to sum up the situation within seconds. They would say things to me but I didn't know if they really meant them. The need for clarity became important to me.

Does that sound far-fetched? When I was a pastor and people talked to me, I asked them to explain statements they made. "I'm not sure what you mean," I would say, or "You lost me there. Would you try it again?"

Perhaps I can show this best in my writing. I don't claim to be the best writer, but rarely do people have to ask, "What did you mean?" If anything I've sometimes overexplained.

When I first began to work with Deidre Knight, my literary agent, I asked many questions. At first, I think she felt I questioned her competence, which I never did. Finally, I explained my need to avoid any ambiguity. "What you do with my book manuscripts and where you send them is up to you. I simply need to know. As long as I'm clear on what's happening, I'm fine."

That insistence may not sound like a big thing, but to me it's extremely important. I need to know. I need to assess the situation.

Perhaps this further explanation will help. Children make sense of their environment by watching and listening. They try to understand the world by playing out what they see and hear. In a happy, healthy environment, children can cope with confusion and ambiguity. They feel they have permission to ask questions, and the adults in their lives behave in fairly consistent ways. If the adult does something that's not consistent, the children may ask, "Why did you do that?" In healthy environments, they receive answers.

Those of us who were abused rarely had that opportunity. We didn't know why adults abused us. We couldn't understand why it was a secret. If it wasn't wrong, why couldn't we talk about it? Why did our abusers threaten us?

We had to function in an irrational world. Instead of receiving answers or reassurances, we fought our way through confusion and pain.

The Mask He Wears

Some books talk about the masks we wear in public. This is even truer with men who were sexually assaulted as children. They don't wear masks consciously, but submerging their true feelings behind a smile makes life safer for them. They can hide behind the grin and say to the world, "I'm happy. I'm happy." Or they hide behind the glare that silently says, "Don't get too close."

One time in our state-sponsored sexual abuse recovery group, Larry said, "I don't know who I am. I'm one person at work; I'm another person in my social life." He named three or four other situations and seriously asked which one was real. And ended with, "And if I knew the real me, would I like me?"

I don't remember the answer but the discussion went on a long time. Today, my answer would be, "They're all you. Some of them have been *you* hiding behind a mask, but they're all you. Even the part of you that hides probably slips out at times."

All of us want to be liked and to be accepted. All of us do things to make people think better of us. I write *all* because I think it's natural to do whatever we can to appear at our best, especially to people we want to influence or to those we want to like us. We don't do it consciously; I assume it's an inborn quality. We want to be significant and important to at least a few people. We probably inherited that from Adam and Eve, and that's a factor in being human.

I met Alvin at least a decade ago. I liked him but he embarrassed me or upset me when we were in a public place. When a pretty woman walked by, for example, he would whistle or make crude remarks about how attractive she was. The women usually heard him—which I suppose was the purpose.

Besides the inappropriateness, Alvin's comments and leers didn't have what I call the ring of truth. They seemed aimed to impress the males with him rather than express actual lust. One time we went on a business trip and spent four days together. The last day I asked him quite bluntly, "Are you afraid I'll think you're gay?"

I shocked him, which I intended to do. He never admitted that was the reason, but he did say that he'd been in a sexual relationship with a man from the time he was fourteen until he was eighteen, ". . . when I finally graduated from high school and left town." He said he hated the sexual part, but he loved being held. "I've never done that again," Alvin said.

At the time we talked, he was fifty-nine years old. He wore a Casanova, sex-crazed mask, but it was a mask. I didn't say so, but I wondered if the mask was for other people or if it was for Alvin.

Masks hide the dark side but they also hide the positive side. Haven't we met people who come across as indifferent or uninteresting, and later we discover that's not who they are at all? By setting up barriers to intimacy, adult survivors keep out the predators, but we also keep out those who want to be friends.

During my early days as a writer, I participated in something called Writers in the Park. We met in Atlanta's Piedmont Park, which hosts many cultural events. I was extremely uncomfortable. I had published three books, all displayed for sale, but I didn't like being there and felt embarrassed because I was there only to sell my books. I watched others smile, shake hands, and talk enthusiastically to people who approached their tables. I'm sure my aloofness is also the reason few people stopped at my table.

Two years later, the woman who had been at the table next to me taught at the same conference as I did. "I like you, and you seem so friendly," she said near the end of the five-day conference.

The way she said it made me wonder what she meant. So I asked.

She brought up Writers in the Park. "You seemed aloof and indifferent," she said.

I wore a mask that day, even though I wasn't aware of it. My aloofness was my way to hide discomfort and embarrassment. All of us have ways to cope with unpleasant situations. In a few instances I've smiled frequently and worked hard to say the right words with exactly the right tone, but that, too, was a mask.

The point is, if we deny the negative parts of ourselves, we also block showing the positive sides. That woman at the conference would have always believed me to be someone who wasn't friendly if we hadn't had a second occasion to get together.

What about those masks? What do they say? I believe they offer clues about the reality behind them. The attitudes or roles we hide behind say something about us—what we'd like to become or what we're afraid we really are.

I read a brief biography of the silent-screen actor Buster Keaton. He was known for his lack of facial expression. According to what I read, Keaton had been beaten frequently in childhood and later said, "I forgot how to smile." That lack of a smile became his trademark—a face with no expression.

But what else did his mask say? I don't want to play mind reader, but I think it's possible it was his way to hide emotions—all emotions—the good and the bad. He had learned it wasn't safe to express his feelings.

Here's one more example. I associated with Rich in a writers' group for three or four months. He made me uncomfortable because of his intolerance for any theological views that differed from his own. In the first writing group he joined, he attacked Marilyn several times for what he called her "naive understanding of Scripture."

I stopped him several times. On one occasion he defended himself and said, "I'm a liberal."

"No you're not," I said. "You're as rigid in your leftist position as you accuse those on the right of being."

I hadn't thought that statement through before I spoke, but after the words came out, I knew they were right. He hid behind the mask of superior theological understanding. He enjoyed throwing out biblical words and correcting any misinterpretation of the Bible—that is, anything that wasn't as he interpreted it.

I thought he was such a sad man. He had to be correct, and he had to prove the others wrong. I often wondered about the home in which he grew up. He didn't give us a chance to know: abruptly he left the group.

I wish he'd stayed and that he would have allowed us to help him remove his mask and open up to us. If he had, that would also suggest that he'd opened up to himself. Instead, he kept his mask firmly in place.

As I said above, at times we all wear masks. They protect us from being hurt or keep at bay those who invade our privacy and try to get too close. Didn't all of us learn to smile in the face of public disappointment? If we received a bad grade in high school when we expected a good one, few of us cried. We didn't want to face the ridicule or embarrassment.

If you can see the masks even in yourself, think about the man in your life who was once abused. He was a vulnerable kid who was hurt, and his childhood was stolen. To cry did no good, so he fortified himself by hiding behind a mask.

The problem is that the mask is just that: it's a facade, a charade, or a pretense. If he stays behind the mask long enough he may actually believe that's who he is. As long as he hides behind the false persona, he won't know his true, deeper self.

And he's probably unaware of his protective mask. He put it on instinctively, and he's probably worn it a long time. He remains in the protective mode so that others won't be able to peek behind the curtain and see what's really there. Others won't be able to see his vulnerability. If they do, he thinks they'll hurt him again and he's already had too much pain.

Think of it this way. What if he began to wear the mask for protection? What if he did it because he was tired of being hurt and it was to insulate himself from torment and pain? If that's true, how can he be truly happy around other people? Someone he trusted violated his trust and injured him. That injured child is the one who secretly says, "If you really knew who I was, you'd hate me."

When he shows his masked face, though, he's probably not even aware that he yearns for someone to pull it away. He wants someone who can look into his eyes and say, "I love the real you."

Long-Term Problems

For men who were sexually assaulted, here are some major long-term effects:

+ Inability to trust others, or they go the other way and naively trust everyone.
+ Self-blame and guilt.
+ Overachievement (or underachievement). He may feel like an imposter if he achieves success.
+ Low self-esteem, negative self-image, feelings of being flawed, bad, or worthless.
+ Discomfort in being touched—or he may constantly and unconsciously touch others.
+ Hypervigilance. He may have an extreme startle response. That is, he'll jump at any unexpected noise or touch.
+ Problems with intimacy. He may be unable to sustain intimacy in relationships or he may enter into abusive relationships where he can be victimized again.
+ Sexual problems that range from dysfunction to promiscuity to compulsion.
+ Substance abuse, depression, and suicidal thoughts and attempts.
+ Symptoms of post-traumatic stress disorder.
+ Unrealistic or negative body images. He may see himself as fat (even if he's not) or ugly (even if he's handsome). He may have no true idea what his body looks like and may feel distant and separated from his own body.

+ Struggle with gender identity, such as attempts to *prove* his masculinity by having multiple female sexual partners or sexually assaulting others. Sometimes these men are confused over their own sexual identities and their adequacy as men. They sense a loss of power, control, and confidence in their manhood. Many fear that their sexual assault has caused (or will cause) them to become homosexual or pedophiles. They may develop an irrational fear of homosexuality.

When the adult survivor no longer needs the mask, he can know he's healed or at least moving ahead in the healing process. He won't have to be afraid; he won't have to hide.

13

MALE SELF-IMAGES

The effects of sexual abuse are, in many ways, similar in both men and women. In both, how the effects show up depends on individual responses. Too often, men see themselves through cultural stereotypes of society. One of the healthiest things for these men is to acknowledge that they are individual creations of God.

One of the things I used to say aloud to myself was, "I am a unique, unrepeatable miracle of God. God will never make another person exactly like me." When I felt a sense of shame or guilt, it helped to say those words aloud to myself.

Each of us is born with the capacity for feelings and for expressing a wide range of human emotions. From the time we are born, however, the human authority figures in our lives begin to teach us how to respond— or not to respond. Part of the enculturation process includes learning the differences between men and women. All cultures have so-called male roles and female roles, although much of that has changed during the past generation.

In the area of sexuality, some of these stereotypical roles still seem to be entrenched in our culture. Our culture expects males to be confident, aggressive, and dominant. Women's roles have changed and have begun to take on more of the so-called male behavior patterns. We men, however, are generally accepted as the arousers and controllers. We chase the females we want. Women, or so our society has taught, are passively swept away by passion. Someone has said, "Sex is like ballroom dancing. The man chooses the partner, the man leads, and the female follows."

Although many of these sexual stereotypes have fallen away, some still exist. We have trouble believing that women can sexually abuse boys—but they do. And our culture doesn't provide a support system for male victims. Men are supposed to deal with circumstances like, well, a man. That is, we're expected to take charge and control the situation.

When a man can't or is unwilling to take control, he is called cowardly, sissy (which is a diminutive of *sister*), effeminate, unmanly, and sometimes even whispers of being gay follow him. In the group of fifteen in which I was involved, one of them said he told his best friend about his abuse. Within days the word had gotten around school "that I was a homo."

As much as we're aware of the lack of logic in macho thinking, most men haven't absorbed or unconsciously internalized the irrationality of it. Male survivors may know that violent revenge would be wrong, would dishonor God, and not be wise. Even so, many of them feel like weaklings for not resorting to violence on some level. Aren't men supposed to be in charge? Many men feel that frustration, fear, and confusion aren't acceptable. "If I were a real man, I'd . . ." Even if he doesn't say those words, he might think them.

If the adult survivor is not like that "real man," what is he? What has the abuse done to him? He doesn't blame the abuser—that comes later—but he sees himself as defective. Thus, victims learn to conceal who they are because of their abusive childhood and for fear of being victimized again. They adapt in many ways to compensate for—and to hide—their assault.

They may conceal themselves by talking. Words for these men become weapons of self-defense, and they often have extensive vocabularies. They were physically powerless to protect themselves, so words prevent others from piercing their fragile defenses.

That sentence describes me. I was a small kid, and several big kids in the neighborhood beat up the smaller kids. I learned early that if I joked with them and was able to get them to laugh, they rarely tried to beat me up.

Twice during childhood, I was threatened by bullies, but my words saved me. When I was in second grade, Bobby Jones was in the same grade but had been held back in first grade and again in second. He was not only two years older than the rest of us, but he was larger. The first time he threatened me he was with his older brother. I asked Bobby to show me his muscles and asked him how he got so muscular. "I'll bet you're the strongest boy in second grade."

He showed me his biceps and told me that he did fifty push-ups every day. I joked about how hard that would be for me. "After five push-ups, I'd fall down and quit," I said.

The second time, Bobby waited for me after school because I had laughed at him in class. (That wasn't kind of me, of course.) I yelled at him, "You can beat me but I'll bite, kick, scratch, and do everything I can. You'll have to kill me to stop me."

In that case, I think I actually scared him. Bobby laughed at me and walked away. He never came after me again. My flurry of words had worked. I couldn't do anything physically to defend myself, but my mouth worked overtime.

Would I have done what I threatened? Probably not, but I was smart enough to know that he could pound with his fists and hurt me.

Another bully, whom I remember only as Skip, said, "Oh, you fight like a girl, do you?"

"I fight any way I can. And no matter what you do to me, you'll probably be blind because I'll scratch out your eyes." This seems silly to put in writing, but I was about seven years old and he was eleven. He never bothered me again.

Words worked.

One time when I was in grad school, I had a private conversation with one of my instructors. I've long forgotten the context, but I can't forget one thing he said. "Do you always cover everything with words? Do you think words make everything right?"

I stared at him because I thought, *What else should I do? What's wrong with that?*

Obviously I didn't get it then. Perhaps that's why the question stayed with me through the years. Words were a useful means of surviving childhood; they're not always a useful method, though, in the adult world.

They may become invisible. They go to a party or to class, and no one knows they're there. They don't speak up and they rarely make eye contact. When they do speak, they're self-effacing. The body language of some men in social situations makes it clear they don't want anyone to talk to them, and they want to become Mr. Invisible.

"It seems that whenever I opened my mouth, I got in trouble," Andy said of his days in three different foster homes. "Not only was there sexual abuse at one of them and verbal abuse at a second one, but it was safer to pull away from everyone. The less they noticed me, the less trouble I had."

They may become the intellectuals. They're the academics and they try to look like it. They may dress in drab clothes and retreat into intellectual discussions. They talk about what they think or observe; they rarely talk about what they feel.

I met August at a small group in a men's conference. I remember that much of his name only because it was unusual. He told me it was short for Augustine, and explained that St. Augustine was a fourth-century theologian. Before I could say anything, he started a lengthy lecture about how Augustine influenced Martin Luther, who influenced others. He never allowed me to say anything of a personal nature.

Even though all of us had been molested, talking to him was the first instance I encountered of a man's coping with abuse by moving totally inside his head. I suppose he was brilliant—I don't know. But he seemed mentally above all the things around him. In our small group, for instance, the leader gave us an exercise to help us open up to each other. We were to talk about a novel we'd read—any novel—and tell the others why we remember it. When August's turn came he said, "I don't read novels. They're an insult to intelligence."

They may become the jokers of the crowd. They often hang around with the tough guys or sometimes become the clown of the in-crowd. They know the latest jokes and have quick replies to everything. No one gets close to them, and they don't let anyone see their pain.

One teen named Barry, who was about my size, hung around in the macho group in school—the black sheep, rebel group. I ran into him one day after graduation, before I'd become conscious of my abuse. I have no idea why, but we started to talk, went to a movie together, and on the way home he told me about being sexually abused. It was the only time I had ever seen Barry outside of class when he wasn't clowning around. I felt sorry for him, but I don't think I ever made contact with him again. I probably wasn't emotionally able to do so.

What I remember more than his words was that he grinned often—even as he told about his most horrendous experience. Even at the time, the grin seemed incongruous to me.

They may become the nice men. They placate. They don't stir up trouble, they care, they help, and they direct attention away from themselves. Nothing seems to upset them, and they become friends with just about everybody—not close friends—but reliable individuals.

In our group sponsored by the state, George was the nice guy. He was easy to get along with, and I don't think he ever caused any problems or said anything significant. When someone became the brunt of comments, he jumped in and said, "Now take it easy on him. We don't want to hurt his feelings."

When anyone asked George a question, he deflected it with a response like, "Oh, you guys know better than I do."

The therapist stared at him near the end of our first meeting and said, "But we want to know what you feel."

George shrugged, and gave a noncommittal response. The therapist pushed him but George didn't give us a real answer. He was one of the first to leave our group; he never returned for the third meeting.

They may become the challengers. They're critical and intolerant and thus push away any personal attacks. In our Georgia group, one man, whose name I can't remember, frequently argued with the therapist. "How do you know that?" was one of his favorite questions.

One time I made a statement about the need to forgive. "When did God appoint you to teach our group?" he asked.

To my surprise, he stayed with the group for almost half of the year. He softened a bit, but not much. The last time he attended, near the end of the meeting the therapist said something like, "You're trying hard to make me dislike you, but it doesn't work. I like you."

The man didn't answer, but he didn't return the following week. That may have been the right thing for him to do. He might not have had the ability to regulate his emotions therapeutically in such a charged atmosphere.

They may become the protectors. That one confused me for a time. But I saw that as adults, abuse victims often look out for the underdog. They jump in when anyone seems attacked. I met one survivor who explained this to me. "We feel that children are in constant danger. I tried to deal with my own molestation and fear by taking on the role of protector."

He came to realize that he tried to give others the protection he hadn't received. He said, "I started as a teacher and now I'm a principal. In my position, I can protect all the kids in the school." He paused and added, "Or at least I try to do that."

After I became involved with other men who'd been abused, I noticed how many of them are involved in the helping professions. In fact, it strikes me as fascinating that they are in various kinds of the human services. I met men who were teachers, ministers, social workers, nurses, and one man who was a lawyer who specialized in abuse cases.

These aren't the only roles adult survivors assume, but they're certainly the ones I've noticed. It would be greatly healing for the man you care for if he could learn to look beyond his behavior patterns and seek the person he is beyond the role he's assumed. With help, he can look for the hurting child, but he needs to know that, with you, he is safe.

14

COMPARTMENTALIZING HIMSELF

In order to survive, many victims of childhood abuse compartmentalize. It's not a conscious choice. I think it's some unconscious internal wisdom that discovers a way to protect us from further pain. If we can throw our hurts into one room and seal it off, we can ignore them. They don't go away, and they may pound against the walls, but they're shut off from our consciousness.

Everyone compartmentalizes to a certain extent. Most people respond differently to friends than to strangers, to children than to adults, but for most individuals the core person remains the same. As adults, people adapt to the requirements of a range of social situations, but they don't deny who they are. The more secure people feel, the more their personalities become integrated. Most people don't have to change who they are to interact with others.

Many abuse survivors, however, have undergone a fundamental change because of the abuse. Many of us can't—or won't—access certain parts of ourselves. It's not just pain we seal off; we who compartmentalize tend to isolate one part of ourselves from other parts. It feels safer. It's easier to act a role if we're first sure of the play into which we've been cast. Until then, the adult survivor believes the less he shares with others, the less likely the abused part will affect other parts of his life. He doesn't realize, though, that abuse influences all parts of himself.

In our state-sponsored group, one of the men said he knew that he'd been sexually molested, but he couldn't get in touch with his feelings.

"It's as if they live in a different country and speak a language I haven't learned."

The lead therapist treated him kindly and didn't push. He encouraged the man to be open to himself. "You hold the key that opens the locked doors," the therapist said. "When you feel safe and you're with people you trust, you'll unlock the door."

Eventually that man opened up. He didn't cry, but his voice broke several times. The therapist commended him. "It took a lot of courage for you to do that," he said.

"I'm still scared."

Spontaneously, two of us walked over and hugged him.

The next week he opened the doors a little wider.

"Once those doors are open," the therapist said, "you expose yourself, and that scares you. Once they're fully open, the fear vanishes. You can begin to accept those parts of yourself that scare you. If you continue to open doors, you'll learn to like and to love every part."

As I watched and listened to the compartmentalized member, I realized something. The more information he gave us about himself, the less control he had over how we could use the information he shared with us. More than once, he spoke of not feeling safe in telling most of his story of abuse. "I feel people can use that to hurt me." When asked how, he said, "By lying about me or avoiding me because they think I'm dirty."

"Do you think there's anyone in this room who would do that?"

He shook his head. "Not really . . . but I'm still scared."

"Of course you are. The change occurs slowly. Be patient with yourself."

I understood something of compartmentalization. Occasionally, bits of information had slipped out, and I worried that people would use it against me. Yet, no one ever did. In time, I came to understand why I worried: information means power. Many of us know that others can use that power to hurt us, and we don't want to supply the ammunition. For me, just that bit of information actually helped to empower me. I could better judge what information to share with whom.

Opening that door is a step toward integration, and most of us abuse survivors find it difficult to integrate our personalities. In my case, I didn't have a role model to follow. The adults who abused me showed one type of personality when they abused me, and a different side when other people were around. As I reviewed my abusive childhood, I think that might be one reason I kept my secrets. I learned to pretend that life was all right, and if I kept silent I survived the sexual abuse from Mr. Lee and from the female relative as well as the physical abuse from my father.

Even as a kid, I grasped that I was different at school than I was at home. Inside our house, I wasn't safe, especially when it was dark. At home, I became quiet and didn't talk much to the rest of the family. I became a reader at an early age, and it was one way for me to shut out the yelling and the chaos of my siblings.

By contrast, at school I was a good student. Most mornings I awakened, eager to get to my classroom. Until I was in ninth grade, I never had a single absence. One time, in fourth grade, my teacher said I had a fever, and sent me to the school nurse in the middle of the morning. The nurse sent me home. At home, my mother gave me an aspirin, and I went right back for the afternoon sessions.

My compartmentalization wasn't as severe as that of others I've met. I think of Henry. He said that he was fine as long as he had to interact with only one person at a time. It didn't matter whether that interaction was in a meaningful relationship—and most of them weren't. That's because meaningful relationships can take unexpected turns, but "if [a relationship] was predictable, it held no [unwelcome] surprises." He also said he could tell lies or shave the truth any way he chose—so long as he remembered what he said.

As Henry pointed out in our state-sponsored group, surprises can be unpleasant and he felt that most of his had been. He also pointed out that the more he kept himself shut off from others, the less he had to share. "If you don't know much about me, you can't hurt me," he said. He looked directly at me when he said those words.

"Why would I want to hurt you?" I asked. "Why would any of us here want to hurt you?"

"How do I know that?" he answered.

The therapist stopped me and said to me, "You're arguing from logic. Relax."

I pulled back, and as I did so, I understood. The more information he let out, the more permission he gave someone to work against him.

"If Henry can keep the abuse stored in a steel box," another member said, "it won't touch other parts of his life. He can keep it under control."

I felt sorry for Henry and tried to talk to him a few minutes after the meeting. We spoke perhaps two minutes before he started to pull away. He said, "I don't want to get close to you—not to any of you."

"That's the second time you've shocked me tonight," I said.

Henry glared at me. "If you have to know, I'm terrified of anyone getting close to me." He pushed away from me and left.

Henry came to another meeting or two. Then the therapist received a letter from him, which said that he'd changed jobs and would no longer be free on Monday evenings. When the therapist read it to the class, we all looked at each other. I don't think one of us believed what Henry wrote.

Perhaps five years later I met Henry again at a social function. We had lunch together occasionally for a couple of years. One time he said, "Cec, you know more about me than anyone else." He looked directly into my eyes. "You're the first man I've ever trusted."

Henry and I are still in occasional contact. He allowed me to use this story, providing I not reveal his name. I respect his privacy, and I honor the privilege of telling his story.

— 15 —

HIS NEED FOR CONTROL

One of the issues the survivor faces is that of control. He may, in fact, feel he must try to control everything in the world around him, and that becomes a daunting task. He has power over himself in certain areas but there are other things over which he has no control, such as the feelings, actions, and attitudes of other people. He doesn't know what will happen tomorrow. He can't change what happened yesterday, but he can heal from the negative effects of his experience.

Bill said that he'd been a Christian as a child, and he left the church when he was a teen. After a failed marriage and his inability to relate to women, he began to deal with his sexual abuse, which he had repeatedly pushed from his mind. He met a woman in church, whom he later married. But before the marriage, she told him that he needed help—she wasn't sure what it was. When he told her he'd been abused, she offered to go to counseling with him.

Bill was shocked that she would be willing to do that. He said it was the first awareness he had of breaking up the compartmentalization.

"God was watching over me," Bill said. "I didn't know it, and for many years I didn't care. But when Bev came into my life, I realized that God was not only in control, but he had plans for my life that I wouldn't have considered."

To relinquish control or to surrender doesn't mean that a man quits trying. It means he has come to face things over which he has no power. It doesn't mean giving up responsibility; it means he understands there are some things beyond his ability to manage. Admitting that reality is, in itself, empowering.

Giving up the attempt to rule our own lives is different for every victim. It may mean admitting the survivor can't cure himself and he decides to seek professional help. It may mean that he can't push away his anger or can't rise above his pain. He can't get past feeling he is bad or evil. But when he opens himself to God, he's taking the first steps toward giving up control. That's saying, "Okay, God, I tried it my way, and it didn't work. Now I hand it over to you to help me."

✦ ✦ ✦

She had been sexually molested as a child in boarding school. One day she told me about it. She said that after she was grown, when she dated and later married (twice), "I controlled the men in my life."

Long after our conversation, I realized the importance of power and control. She had to be in control because power was what she didn't have as a child. As I pondered her words, I began to grasp how important power was for her. She said it had taken her years to get past that and to trust men.

I understood because it works the same way with many men. It intrigued me that she had such a clear picture of her need to be in the power position. It's not always easy for us to recognize the effects of our own sexual abuse. Especially, it's often difficult to see cause-and-effect in behavior.

✦ ✦ ✦

Again, I want to share a lesson I learned from my experience. I'm fairly outgoing and like being around people. I like to engage others in conversation. But one day I realized that I did more than engage: I controlled. As long as I kept the conversation moving along safe lines, I relaxed. Did I do that consciously? Of course not. Had I been aware, I would have changed earlier.

I became aware of the need to keep conversation *safe* one Wednesday evening. At the time, Shirley was an editor with our denominational publishing house, and I had left the pastorate to become a full-time writer. We belonged to a group of publishing professionals—writers, editors, proofreaders, artists—any position that had to do with publishing. We had monthly dinner meetings.

We met at a restaurant that set us at tables of eight. Shirley wasn't able to attend that particular meeting, but I was there. Within minutes after we started our informal discussion before the evening speaker, I realized that I controlled the conversation. It wasn't that I talked so much but that I pushed the conversation in the directions I wanted it to go. I cracked a joke or made a comment that steered us into safe waters. I made certain everyone had a chance to speak—another method to keep the conversation in control. I was the one who said, "What do you think, Jim?" "How do you feel about that, Betty?"

Nothing was amiss. No one talked on heavy topics or got into areas of abuse or anything that related to my personal issues. Yet in the middle of that half-hour period I realized what I was doing. It hit me like a sharp blow to my head. I stopped and didn't speak again. It was a lively group, and I doubt that anyone noticed. As I sat in silence and smiled at appropriate times, my mind focused on the matter of control. I realized that this particular discussion hadn't been the first time I'd managed the conversation. In fact, it was the pattern. I felt ashamed of myself but I said nothing.

After the meeting, I sat in my car in the parking lot for a long time, trying to figure out what had happened to me. What made me act that way? At first, nothing seemed to make sense, and then I got it: in some unexplainable way I was making up for my lack of power and control as a child. Abuse wasn't near my consciousness yet, but I was probably getting emotionally ready.

Instead of *control*, I began to use the word *power* or *domination*. I admitted to myself that for most of my life—from my teens through adulthood—it was something I had exerted naturally. No one had ever accused me of dominating, and I think it was because I didn't do all the talking. I jumped in when I unconsciously sensed we neared a dangerous spot in the road. I was the kid who rallied behind ideas or groups.

Controlling a discussion is not a direct line to childhood abuse, but on that Wednesday night, I saw the link to my childhood. In that epiphany, I realized that, as a child with no power and no ability to protest or to say no, I had burst forth with my own version of power.

I remembered that by the time I was in third grade, I'd realized the power of words. I recognized that some part of me had twisted things around so that I was able to dominate and bring others into agreement with what I wanted. (Not always, of course, but many times.) *I needed to dominate.* I like to think that my domination was benign, but it was an unconscious way to push away the pain to which others had subjected me.

I confess it still happens occasionally, that I control conversations, but less frequently than before. The reason it happens less often is that I don't *need* to dominate. The more I experience healing, the less I need to control. It means I trust myself, and I trust that others won't hurt me.

For the adult survivor, the need to dominate may not show itself in words. It might be more evident in actions or even in lack of interest. An important step in healing, though, may be a recognition of the behavioral patterns.

16

WHAT ABOUT BOUNDARIES?

Sexual abuse involves the violation of personal boundaries. Even as adults, many abused men don't understand the word *boundaries*. Remember, his personal life was invaded and violated in childhood. Men who were once molested tend to go one of two ways: either they don't want to tell anybody about the abuse or they seem to want to tell anyone who will listen.

It's the second response that I want to address. As one person said, "I had no sense of propriety. I tended to blab my story to anybody who would listen."

When he began to deal with his past, naturally his abuse was the subject that occupied his mind. It was the most important thing in his world at that time. What had been a carefully guarded secret, he now told everyone. It became a source of relief to tell it.

I was well into my recovery before I heard someone use the word *boundaries*. For several days I thought about the issue. I hadn't set boundaries and didn't know how to go about implementing them. As a child, my perpetrators had disrupted any sense of personal privacy.

It took me awhile to grasp the concept. Someone said that a boundary is the place you say the word *end* and the other person says *begin*. Boundaries define our personal space, emotionally and geographically. They develop as we mature and learn who we are, and they define our relationship with other people.

Growing up, most of us abused boys had little idea of boundaries. Whatever we learned in childhood became our limits. Because some older, more powerful person invaded his personal space, an adult survivor might be uncertain about where to set limitations today.

One way of not understanding the limitations of others in my life showed up when anyone asked me a question. I gave the truest answer possible. Even if the question was inappropriate, I replied. Sometimes I didn't like the question, but I didn't question the person's right to ask.

The first time I recall resenting anyone for asking questions was when I became pastor of a church and "inherited" a secretary. She worked hard and was generally agreeable, but when I prepared to leave the office, she wanted to know where I was going, how long I'd be gone, and whom I would see. If I simply said, "I'm going to the hospital," she wanted to know which one (we had seven in our general area) and which patients I would visit.

It put me in a difficult position. One part of me wanted to tell her everything simply because she'd asked. That's what seemed right to me because no one had taught me how or when to say no. Another part of me resented her intrusion, resented her treating me as if I were an irresponsible child. It wasn't any of her business, and she didn't need to know in order to do her job. Until then, it hadn't occurred to me that I didn't owe people an explanation.

The second or third time it happened, I said, "Is that how your mother or father treated you? Always insisting on knowing everything when you left?"

"My dad was that way," she said, and she obviously didn't make the connection or have any idea that she'd moved into my personal space.

"You're not my dad," I said in as calm a voice as I could and walked out of the office. She sulked the next time I was ready to leave but I was determined that she didn't need to know every detail of the next two hours. I was willing to let her know I was going out and when I would return; sometimes I told her my destination, sometimes not. She worked for me for two years and didn't like my "curt responses," as she called them, but she didn't challenge me again.

I have to confess, however, that it was a painful victory. I knew I was right, but I felt guilty. On two different occasions I started to apologize to the secretary but I stopped myself. Though I didn't understand it at the time, I was changing the rules of my life. Later, I realized that once we start on the healing journey, the first steps may evoke negative feelings such as guilt.

Family Dynamics

As I've reviewed my life within the past few years, I realize that my family atmosphere set things up for the lack of personal boundaries.

There was no respect for personal boundaries within our family. Nothing was exclusively mine, even if I bought it with my own money. If I received a letter and hid it somewhere, it didn't matter because someone within the family would likely find it. If someone else found it, that seemed to give that person the license to read it. A closed door meant nothing. The only privacy we had was when we locked a door.

When I was twelve I bought a bicycle by delivering newspapers in the morning and working as a delivery boy three afternoons after school. My younger brother, Mel, took my bicycle whenever he wanted to. I finally bought a padlock, which was the only way I could keep him from using it.

Our parents didn't teach us coping skills. Our parents didn't argue. In fact, they didn't talk to each other. I don't think they ever raised their voices to each other. Dad, in fact, didn't talk to any of us about anything except to give us orders or to criticize what we'd done. We had few rules spelled out for us, and thus no boundaries.

I learned interpersonal skills from observing school friends, reading books, and watching movies. Even so, I lacked many interpersonal skills, and one of them was how to say no. When Mr. Lee molested me, I didn't like it but I didn't know how to refuse or who to tell. How could I know in a family like ours?

We had no discussion about sex. The most I recall was that my parents spoke of a woman being "that way" to indicate pregnancy. There was certainly no discussion about putting hands where they don't belong, and I would never have brought up abuse within the family. My older sister told on the pedophile who abused us both, but I couldn't have done that.

We lived in a "blame atmosphere." When someone did something wrong, such as leaving the kitchen light burning all night, as soon as we discovered the culprit, he or she was usually punished, and that was the end of it. I don't recall ever being commended for doing something right; I vividly recall being punished for doing wrong. In such an atmosphere, I learned what fear is, and fear caused me to shield myself.

For many of us abused males, boundaries rank high on our lists of things we're confused about. Where, and about what subjects, do we draw the line? I've gotten better at recognizing, and refusing to let people barge into, my private space.

The man in your life may face the same issues. When he was molested, it meant someone stepped over the line, invaded his private world, and left havoc behind. As bad as it is for adults to have someone cross the line, it's more traumatic for children. Their limits haven't been fully formed and it leaves them confused.

When someone asks a question—whether appropriate or inappropriate—to answer honestly is an excellent rule. But what if honesty will injure another? I was thirty years old before someone said to me, "You don't have to tell them everything you know." As odd as that sounds, it came to me as a startling revelation. I hadn't learned to withhold. Today, it's not that I lie, but I know how and what information to withhold, as most people do.

I also realized that I agreed to do favors for others that I didn't want to do. They asked, and it didn't occur to me to refuse. On the few occasions when I did, I needed to give a long justification and a deep-felt apology.

Not having clear boundaries robs us of a strong sense of self. We don't know who we are. It also means that others define us. As we move into freedom, we learn that powerful, invaluable word.

I also want to say that my wife taught me the best lessons about boundaries. It took me years to get it. One day, for example, a woman asked Shirley to do her a favor.

"No," Shirley said, smiled, and started to walk away.

"Why not?" the shocked woman asked.

In a soft voice, my wife said, "You asked me and I told you no. Do I owe you an explanation?"

"I guess not," the woman said.

As Shirley and I walked away, I wished I could do that.

I can now, but it took many years.

Developing Relationships

How does being unsure about boundaries work out in developing relationships? Usually it means that, as an adult survivor, a man may allow people to constantly invade his private space and take advantage of him. That was the dynamic he grew up in. Or he may have trouble developing into an independent, self-determined individual. He may allow others to influence him, and he may act on their wishes and not on his own. He might have invested himself so fully in others, he has neglected his own needs and desires. In effect, he has no sense of boundaries.

Perhaps five years after I'd been in recovery, I asked myself, "What do I want?" I didn't know. For most of my life I'd catered to others' wishes and needs. I don't mean I was selfless, only that I focused so much on what others wanted, I didn't consider what I wanted. In the family I grew up in, for instance, my obvious-but-unspoken role was that of caregiver. I was the one who brought peace, the one the family could rely on to act. When Dad died, I saw that clearly. Although I lived about nine hundred miles away, the family deferred to me to make the decisions. I had six siblings, and not one of them could pick out a casket. Within hours after my arrival, six of us went to the funeral home and within five minutes, I'd selected the casket.

That illustration nudges me to think of my career pattern. As I look back, is it any wonder I chose the professions I did? I taught public school a couple of years, taught part-time in college for eighteen years, and was a missionary and pastor for about twenty. Even though it's been a long time since I left the pastorate to write full time, my wife has said several times, "You may not have a church, but you're still a pastor."

That's the role I know; that's the role I've lived. That's part of who I am today. It's not a bad thing. The problem was that I did it *unconsciously*. Sometimes I felt I had no choice in the matter. I believe God called me to those places, but I also believe that my family background pushed me, in serving, to overlook my own welfare. And because I had little sense of what Cec wanted, the ministry was where I went.

Another effect of invaded privacy and overstepped boundaries is that some of us have tended to disclose too much personal information about ourselves. Sometimes those we've told have later used that information to hurt us. Or we may have gone the other way, erecting a wall between others and ourselves. People could come close but not too close. Because we didn't understand boundaries, we held up a NO TRESPASSING sign to everyone.

Another effect is to idealize anyone who is kind and caring, anyone who seems to like us. I can relate my own experience, because I was the idealist. Although it wasn't easy for me to trust, when I did meet someone who got close to me, I idealized that person and could see only the good in him or her.

I became aware of my idealism when I was in my mid-twenties. We had a pastor named Art. Even before we joined his congregation, my wife's uncle had asked him to come to our house to pray for me. I'd had extensive dental work and remained in pain with a fever for a full day.

Art was warm and compassionate. At the time, we were church shopping. After we met Art, Shirley and I didn't visit another church. For months, as I sat in the congregation and listened, I felt as if every message he preached was just for me. He organized a prayer group that met at six in the morning twice a week. I joined and didn't miss. Some mornings only Art and I showed up. We prayed and often walked together.

One time in referring to me, Art quoted the apostle Paul when he spoke of Timothy, his spiritual son, saying there was no one else quite like him: "I have no one like-minded" (Phil. 2:20 NKJV). That was the highest spiritual compliment I had ever received. It nurtured me for a long time.

One day another man in the church, about my age, named Jack, told me something. He had become active in the church and involved in a number of activities. "You know what Art said to me yesterday?"

When I said I didn't know, he quoted the same message that Art had given me. To my credit, I said nothing. I was too shocked at the time, but that killed something inside of me: my idealism about Art. He had lied. Or perhaps he hadn't, but a lie was the only thing I could call it. In those days, something was totally right or absolutely wrong. After that, I became cynical about him, ready to point out to my wife any flaws I saw in him—and they became quite evident to my critical eye.

As the end to that story, I realized how I related to older men. If they were kind and open, I idealized them. Once they stopped being perfect, I lost respect for them. That revelation wasn't the beginning of a full healing, but it did help me face that particular problem—a problem that is part of setting the proper boundaries for myself and with others.

17

TO FEEL AGAIN

"How do you feel?" If you ask that question of the man you care about, he may have no idea how to answer. Or he may say, "Fine. Good." Those are safe, conventional answers. It's probably not an attempt to be evasive, but for the adult survivor, it's likely an honest, straightforward response. It's his way to say, "I don't know."

If he grew up not feeling his emotions, denying or repressing them, it's likely a habit today. To face his deep-seated feelings can be one of the most painful aspects of his healing process. Yet one of the first rewards of his doing so will be the release of his pain and pressure. Facing the pain and what caused it will also provide opportunities to unlearn destructive behavior patterns and to raise his level of self-esteem. Additional rewards are better communication, fewer arguments.

Denial

When the male survivor was a child, hiding his feelings protected him from the emotional pain of molestation. As a child, it was easier for him to deny his feelings than to face the reality of what happened to him. He didn't consciously repress those feelings—he wouldn't have known how—but it was a protective device, an escape route he learned in childhood.

Many of us carried into adulthood the coping strategies that we developed as children to control or accommodate the abuse. We developed individual feeling-avoidance patterns. Some men have said that as molested children they learned to escape their bodies through their imaginations. Our bodies and minds disconnected, so it was as if we had no knowledge or recollection of what was happening to us. That was true of me. Some of us learned that if we showed any feelings, we got beaten or laughed at.

The saddest men are those who became so disconnected they are still unaware today of how they feel. Some, for example, reason away their feelings: "I had a conventional happy childhood." I've already mentioned that I said those words many times. I answered that way not to avoid or deny, but I had no access to my emotions. I gave as honest an answer as I could. Until I gained access to my emotions, I didn't know how I felt. Whenever I became overwhelmed with emotions—strong feelings that I couldn't process—I numbed out.

Here's another personal example of separating self from emotions. When our children were small, Shirley and I were involved in a head-on collision. I stayed in the emergency room all night with her because the doctor said he didn't expect her to live through the night. She experienced a miraculous recovery, but I sat in the room, staring at her body. Sometimes she moaned. Her face was cut and she had IVs and tubes everywhere. How did I respond? I felt absolutely no emotion. I was fully aware of her condition, and I knew what was going on around me, but I was deprived of emotional response. In the middle of the night as I sat there, I asked God why I was so unfazed by her situation. I couldn't understand. I loved Shirley, and I knew I loved her. So why couldn't I cry? Or feel sad?

It was because I had no access to my emotions. Only after I began the healing process did I begin to move past that numbing effect. Once I realized how that separation worked, when we faced another serious situation I could at least offer a response. I said to Shirley, "I don't feel anything. I don't feel because it's my protective covering shielding me." I wanted to cry. I wanted to fall apart, but I didn't know how. I no longer have that problem, but it was present most of my life.

Some adult survivors medicate their pain as another way to keep the feelings away from the surface. I'm convinced that was true with my two younger brothers. Sunk in the oblivion of alcohol, they didn't feel pain, and they couldn't remember what had been done to them.

A few months before my brother Mel died he called me regularly—usually at 2:00 in the morning. Sometimes his words didn't make sense, but occasionally he broke through enough to carry on a conversation. One time he said, "I want to quit drinking but I can't." I said something about his being addicted and he said, "Yeah, but when I don't drink, I hurt inside." Just that much and he was back into rambling sentences.

Chuck, the baby of the family, once said to me that "a few drinks" mellowed him. He said it stopped the buzzing inside his head. I wonder if that was a way of saying it pushed back the memories.

Some men have done the work of forgetting so successfully that they have no idea how they feel. They don't know if they're happy or sad. By contrast, I've met abused men who cry over what seems like an insignificant matter. They'll weep convulsively when they watch a sad film or they can't stand to look at a hurting animal. They can't focus their emotions on themselves—it may bring too much pain—but they unconsciously transfer the pain toward something outside themselves.

Regardless of how the adult survivor responds, for him to confront his feelings is important for his healing. He needs to become aware of his emotions *now*, because his feelings can enable him to move at his own pace in going back and reliving the pain he felt *then*. If he wants total healing, he will have to go back to that pain at some point. By re-experiencing the pain one more time, he can be freed from it. He can also examine the feeling-avoidance patterns that he followed to survive childhood.

Shortly after I began to recover, I prayed these words every day: "God, help me feel my emotions. I want to feel my feelings." At one point I was afraid that if I felt my emotions, violent anger would erupt. I wondered if I might actually try to kill someone. As illogical as it sounds to me now, I was afraid.

Anger

My anger burst out after I saw a film about a woman who was raped. Later, she had a gun and planned to kill the man. In an emotional scene, she finally walked away and said to him, "You have to live with what you did. You'll never be happy." It was a contrived ending, but in watching it, I became so enraged I felt I could have killed that rapist myself. It was the most violent I'd felt in my adult life. I was afraid to unleash my angry feelings.

When I talked to my friend David, he smiled before he said. "You haven't killed anyone yet. What makes you think you're going to do it if you allow anger to come back to you?" Those words from David freed me. I didn't have to fear my anger.

All of us deal with our emotions differently. Feelings are physical and psychological reactions to events that tell us how those events affected us. They aren't intellectual experiences. They're something that's part of our bodies: they can be a nervous stomach, shallow breathing, tension in the chest, or heavy perspiration.

Anger is a common and powerful emotion that seems generally acceptable for males to feel in our culture. It is normal to feel anger in reaction to a grossly abnormal situation. It's common to abuse victims because someone has violated our trust. Some children aren't allowed to express anger and they stuff it inside. That doesn't mean it's gone; it's there and it slips out in cynicism, rudeness, harsh words, or passive-aggressive ways.

Closing Off

We usually learn about anger through our families. Many abused boys weren't allowed to show anger or to express negative emotions. This seems especially true if they were kids who tried to tell about their abuse and weren't believed. Or they didn't talk because they had no assurance they would be believed. Consequently, the abuse victim may not know how he feels. He may not come across as expressionless and lifeless, but his emotions might be beyond his awareness, especially in traumatic moments.

When we think about sexual molestation, a child's closing of his emotions makes sense, doesn't it? Some of us survived by not feeling, by shutting off our pain, and by blocking out reality. As we move into recovery, we want to feel our emotions. We want to connect our minds and our feelings. Connecting with our inner feelings—whether sadness, pain, or fear—isn't easy. I've spoken with men who have gone through horrendous experiences but don't seem able to feel the hurt. They can describe an event, but it's as if they are observers.

There's no one way, of course, that such a man can become aware of his feelings. Before he is able to connect with his feelings about his molestation, however, he needs to connect to his feelings about other events that are, by comparison, less painful. Early in my recovery, for instance, when I was a member of a six-man group, I told them about a certain editor. I felt this man had taken advantage of me. I shared the experience and said I had been upset, "but I forgave him."

"You haven't forgiven him," John said. When I started to deny it, he said he could see it on my face. I'm not sure what he saw, but apparently the others did too. They also agreed with John. I had to do serious soul searching. They could tell from my facial expressions, or perhaps just my voice, that I still had bad feelings. They could see emotions that remained hidden from me.

Saying the Words

For many adult survivors, to say in words how we feel is difficult. We had to live a deceptive life. We had to pretend everything was all right in our childhood when it was chaotic. We learned to suppress the reality of our feelings.

The pain is deep and the healing journey is long. But if we abused males have caring people to guide us, we can arrive at the destination of experiencing our own emotions.

Once I began my recovery, I prayed every morning, "Lord, help me feel my emotions." I slowly learned to feel my anger. That was the beginning. Emotional awareness slowly surfaced.

I learned something else about feelings that helped in my relationship with Shirley. After I began to feel, I also assumed I expressed my emotions. I was mistaken.

One Sunday morning while Shirley and I drove to church, I poured out my heart about a problem. She nodded but didn't respond. Finally I said, "I'm dripping with emotion in this situation and you seem indifferent."

Shock covered her face. "I didn't realize you were hurting. I thought you were reporting an incident."

For a moment I felt hurt; I'd made myself vulnerable and she heard it only as my telling her about something going on. Before I said anything, though, I realized that if Shirley didn't get the correct message, something was wrong with my transmission. Despite the depth of my pain, the words had come out in code. I tried again, and she understood.

I realized that although I'm long past most of the pain and the drama of recovery, sometimes I fall into old patterns. Shirley and I have since developed a formula. When I have a strong emotional reaction and want to make certain she gets it, I'll say, "I'm not reporting. This is something about which I feel strongly."

That simple statement does two things. First, it helps Shirley to hear me—even if she has to strain to catch the emotion. Second—and for me this is even more important—my own words enable me to open up and to feel what I mean. As I get in touch with what I feel, I can express the emotions more clearly.

One friend told me that he learned to say to his wife, "I feel sad because I've had flashbacks about my abuser. And it makes me feel insignificant when you move around or do things while I talk. I feel as if you're not really listening to me." Just simple statements like that can make a tremendous difference in the relationship.

Dan used to talk out loud to himself. In the grocery store, he'd mumble, "I feel irritated that this line is so long." Or we'd be in his car and he'd say, "I'm angry at that driver who cut me off." It worked for him in two ways because he was learning to both identify and verbalize his negative feelings.

Words, though, aren't the only ways that people communicate feelings. Each person has individual ways of expressing feelings. Some men express their emotions by their behavior. They might cry, but say nothing or become taciturn. They might become physically active.

If the adult survivor can learn to recognize that a certain behavior may indicate a certain emotion, he will be better able to express that emotion. When his breathing becomes quick and shallow, for example, he may be frightened or angry. Stomach tension may mean he's tense or unsure. Once he's become accustomed to expressing his emotions, he won't stop having feelings, but he can stop having so many bad feelings, which might be what troubles him most.

After an awareness of my feelings first surfaced, for a time I responded to everything with exaggerated emotions. Actually, it only seemed that way. I'd lived without awareness of my emotions for so long that when they came to the surface, they felt unusual and strong. As I learned, the big fear was to feel the pain of the past. Once I felt it, I began to do something—anything—to overcome the overwhelming pain.

In time, the intensity of the pain will diminish. As it diminishes, we can get more in touch with our bodies and our behaviors. For the adult survivor, learning to identify and communicate his feelings and learning to feel comfortable in expressing them takes time. It takes commitment and practice.

Feelings and Reality

Concerning reality, for a time, if something *felt* wrong or painful to me, I assumed it to be true: *This is wrong and painful.* I didn't question my conclusion. I think this reaction is typical of men who deal with the emotional effects of abuse.

In a social gathering, for example, I might feel someone had intentionally ignored me. Because I felt that way, it made it so. But sometimes I was wrong. Again, this is where prayer came in. Here's a simple prayer I prayed for years—and still pray daily: "God, help me to know that my feelings are only emotions. My emotions are not reality."

Those two sentences have done a great deal for me. Because I feel something, it doesn't make that feeling a reality. I might be feeling ignored by someone but that other person didn't, in fact, see me. Or perhaps he passed me by to introduce himself to a stranger and would come back to me. It didn't matter. What mattered is that I felt a certain way. Now, whenever possible, I try to get a reality check. I turn to my wife and ask, "Did he purposefully ignore me?"

Survival Behavior

Abused kids can't trust their feelings. They don't have the opportunity to gain perspective. They have no one to trust to make them see that a situation is wrong or that their feelings are acceptable. Some kids don't even know they're abused. I met a fellow named Jake who was beaten regularly during his childhood. He assumed every kid was beaten. That was his experience and no one explained to him that it wasn't normal.

And yet, we abused kids knew something was wrong—even though we couldn't figure out what it was. The world was confusing, adults were inconsistent, and no one helped us understand. Because we had to depend on our own resources, we worked out explanations for what was being done to us, and most of us came to an obvious conclusion: *Something is wrong with me.* We assumed we were flawed or bad. We developed skills just to survive, and they remained with us into adulthood. Some of those ways might be dysfunctional for an adult, but they were survival skills for the victim during childhood.

All people, as we grow from infancy and dependence toward adulthood, come up with an understanding of how the world operates. In normal situations, children have adult help and guidance and positive correction. Men who were abused as boys, with their limited experience and reasoning power, had to figure it out on their own. It wasn't safe to depend on adults. Adults let them down, lied to them, or ignored them. They started life in a hostile world, receiving incorrect information, and with limited mental and emotional resources. They need to be commended for surviving in a hostile environment. Some of their behaviors may seem bizarre to observers but make sense to those men who were molested.

As an example not related to abuse, in seventh grade, I ate in the cafeteria and my friend Rodney ate his dessert first. When I asked why, he said, "I'm the youngest at home, and I don't always get any, but if I grab dessert first, I get it." It was strange, but it made sense to him.

The strange behavior of abused kids is functional, and it enabled us to survive childhood pain. So we need to commend children who find creative ways to struggle through childhood. But some of those childhood survival strategies turn into adult problems. And the survivors blame themselves for creating the problems, and the self-blame provides them even more evidence of their deficiencies.

The victim is not to blame, of course, but rather his behavior was learned as a brave, struggling child who figured out a way to make it through the morass and pain. He deserves admiration and love. He negotiated a way out of insanity and did it even when he wasn't aware of what he did.

He survived childhood, but now he needs to know that change is possible. A loving, safe environment can promote change. He wants to be more than a survivor. He wants to be victorious.

18

FACING HIS ABUSER

"Why must I make peace with the man who molested me?" The first time I heard that question it came from Tim, an extremely angry man. We attended a special meeting of about fifty men in Louisville.

That evening we had an invited speaker who talked on the topic of healing from any form of abuse. He divided us into groups of ten and asked us to talk about making peace with the perpetrator. I was in the same group with Tim, and the vehemence of his words shocked me.

"I might want to kill him, but I sure don't want to kiss him." Several men yelled and clapped.

"No one said anything about kissing," someone answered. "He meant standing up to him and telling him how he ruined your childhood."

"People who molest aren't capable of acknowledging what they did," Tim said. It was obvious that he was still hurting. I think most of us sensed that.

"After I became an adult," Tim said, "I went back to my neighborhood." He tried to get the man from across the street to admit to abusing him. The man denied it. "He said I had always been a nasty kid and he had only tried to be kind to me. He swore at me and said I paid back his kindness with accusations."

We discussed the issue in our group for a few minutes, and many of us had strong feelings about it.

"The problem with my abuser," Tim added, "was that I don't think he was capable of understanding the damage he had done in my life."

"I know how that goes," someone else said. "When I confronted my uncle, he finally admitted something had happened, but he insisted that he did it only because I wouldn't leave him alone."

Another man said, "My abuser insisted I seduced him." He laughed before he said, "I think it was a dumb idea to confront him."

In my case, both of my abusers had been long dead, so I didn't enter into the discussion. As I listened, I asked myself, *If either of them were alive, how would I handle it?*

I decided that I'd probably try to confront Mr. Lee. And then I asked myself, *Why?* What would be the purpose of the confrontation? If it was to get him to admit his sin—and it was sin—I thought that was unrealistic. If it was to get him to apologize, again I don't think he would have.

He knew what he had done to me. And I wasn't the only child. He had also molested my sister, and that probably meant there had been many others. I felt sorry for Mr. Lee. That is, the adult part of me did. I'd come a long way before I was able to have such feelings.

I thought of Mr. Lee for a few minutes while the others talked. I was no older than six when the abuse took place, so I don't remember much about him, but he had to have been an extremely miserable person. How could he not have been? He may have derived pleasure out of the acts of abuse, but he couldn't possibly have been a happy person. I assume he was like a drug addict; he derived momentary pleasure from his "fix," but it didn't last. He would soon have to find another victim.

One of the men in our discussion group, Leonard, decided he'd write a letter to his abuser but not send it. I thought that would be helpful. Leonard and I had coffee together a few days later, and he read it to me.

Two good things came out of that. First, Leonard expressed his pain—and it was an abuse that had gone on about once or twice a week for three years. For him to write out his feelings had to be therapeutic. While reading it aloud, he paused several times to wipe away tears.

Second, I listened to Leonard and understood. I expressed my sympathy. That also furthered my own healing as well as his. Leonard came from a Catholic background, although he'd been inactive in the church. He said that for him to tell me, for me to listen and to respond with sympathy and compassion, felt as good for him as going to confession. "Someone else finally heard my pain. You felt what I felt," he said. "This is the most honest I've ever been able to be about my abuse."

Another man, Jerry, bought a cassette recorder (that was before digital). Each night before he got ready for bed, he went into his office and closed the door. The closed door meant no interruptions from his wife or children. He spoke into the recorder. "Because no one else would ever hear this, I held nothing back." He went on to say that if he had the slightest suspicion anyone would hear, he couldn't have been able to speak so honestly.

He played back the message several times, and each time he changed the message. After a month he was able to speak softer words into the recorder, and eventually he felt he was able to forgive his perpetrator.

In those days I kept a journal, writing in it every day, and did essentially the same thing as Jerry. I told my wife and children that if anything happened to me, they were to burn my journals. They were only for my personal therapy. They understood and promised. In 2007, our house burned down and we lost every possession—including my journals. Sometimes I wish I had them to refer to, but I wrote them back then, read them once afterward, and moved on. They were an important part of my healing, but I don't need them now.

I'm one of those individuals who must talk so I know what I feel. As I wrote in my journal, things came to me that I hadn't consciously thought about for years. I probed as deeply as I could. Because I knew it was safe, I found the experience helpful. In the first year, my journal ran more than three hundred computer pages—most years, the journal ran eighty to ninety pages.

Charlie did an interesting thing. He went for walks in the dark, late in the evenings. While he walked, he envisioned himself as an adult facing his abuser. He talked to his perpetrator and imagined the response. "Sometimes he asked me to forgive him," Charlie said. "In most of my scenarios he denied he had done anything or else tried to say it wasn't important.

"Sometimes I punched him out; sometimes I yelled at him and told him to get out of my life forever. A few times I cried."

For about a year that was Charlie's routine. "I had so much hatred built up inside, I had to find a way to let it out." About the second month of his walk, Charlie walked inside the fence of the local high school's soccer field. It was situated so that he could see anyone approaching long before that person got close to the field.

"It was perfect for me." He said he could yell and kick and do almost anything without being observed. For Charlie, that method worked. Eventually he was able to free himself of the venom. He calls himself "a serious believer," and his spiritual commitment pushed him to work on resolving the issues within his own heart.

✦   ✦   ✦

The experts have told me—and victims themselves have agreed—that perpetrators rarely admit their actions. Some shrug off the abuse as a minor incident. "It happened only a couple of times, and it wasn't a big deal."

Some say, "Yes, we had an affair, but I ended it." By using the word *affair*, it sounds like something mutually consensual.

In my investigation and experiences in this area, I've met only one person who admitted to sexually abusing children. Hank told me a long story of his father abusing him, and he had followed the pattern with his own son. About that time, Hank went back to the church he had left as a teen. He became involved in the local church and eventually had a powerful conversion experience. He apologized to his son and begged his forgiveness. Hank said I was only the fourth person he had ever told about being a perpetrator. "I hated myself for a long time for what I had done. My son has forgiven me. He was kinder to me than I'm able to be to myself."

Of the men I know who actually confronted their abusers, none of them had a satisfactory resolution. They asked questions such as, "Why did you do it? Why did you pick me?"

"I'm not sure it makes any difference to confront the person who molested me," Adam said. "What would I expect to get out of it?" He explained that he had heard others' stories and had read about men who tried. "To do that means we have an agenda. We want an apology from them. Even if we get it, which we probably won't, so what?"

"An apology doesn't undo anything," Thomas said in agreement. "[Seeking an apology would] put me back into trying to undo the past, and I can't change what's already been done." He turned to the group and asked, "Have you ever had success in facing your abuser?"

None received satisfaction in facing their perpetrators or knew of any men who had. "I know guys who've yelled and screamed and accused," one of them said. "They demanded some type of confession the person wasn't willing to make."

For me, I was finally able to say that Mr. Lee was only a miserable man. What must it be like to be controlled by some terrible lust? He had to have been a driven man for him to hurt my sister and me and probably others.

+ + +

If the adult survivor feels that he must personally confront his perpetrator, he needs to prepare himself.

First, he needs to be sure what results he wants.
Does he want an apology?
Does he want reconciliation?
Does he seek some form of restitution?
Is he willing to forgive if the perpetrator asks for it?
If the perpetrator denies his actions, is he still willing to forgive? (See more on this in the next chapter.)

Second, he needs to know what he wants to say. Perhaps he might even have a few notes with him. It might be a powerful, confrontational experience, and he might be so traumatized he'll forget what he wanted to say. Or he may find himself regressing to the way he was as a child. Here are a few things he might want to discuss:

"I asked you to meet with me because . . ."

"I remember when . . ."

"I felt . . ."

"The abuse affected me . . ."

Third, he needs to remember that his healing won't come from the abuser. His healing must come from within—from the grace of God at work in his heart. He needs to be able to forgive the sinner regardless of the other's actions or attitude.

Fourth, if he meets face-to-face with the abuser, it needs to be safe. He needs to choose the location, making sure it's either a neutral place or at least not the perpetrator's home. He needs to insist on a place where he feels safe. He might want to take along a friend—if that's agreeable.

Fifth, he needs to be prepared to hear denials and excuses.

"You're out of your mind. I never did anything wrong with you. Not ever."

"Yes, but it happened only once [or a few times]."

"It wasn't a big thing. It was just sex."

"You enjoyed it then. What happened to you?"

Sixth, he needs to avoid allowing the abuser to sidetrack him. The perpetrator might try to defend sex between adults and children as a good thing. I once heard about a perpetrator who did that. The victim refused to debate the issue. He didn't get satisfaction from the perpetrator, but he said, "At least I got it off my chest."

Seventh, as soon as possible afterward, he should talk to someone he trusts. This may be the significant woman in his life, a therapist, or someone else he trusts. He needs to be able to process the encounter with someone who can listen uncritically.

For his own inner peace, the adult survivor may feel that he absolutely must confront his abuser. Talking to other survivors or a counselor—someone with experience—will help give him perspective and enable him to handle the situation wisely.

19

FORGIVING HIS ABUSER

Who doesn't know we need to forgive those who have sinned against us? Even nonbelievers understand that forgiveness is a strong element in the Christian faith. Although no believer disagrees, that doesn't make forgiving easy.

In the case of abuse, forgiveness is not for the well-being of the perpetrator; it is for the benefit of the former victim. That is, we forgive for our own sakes. We forgive so we're not burdened and constantly angry over what others did to us. The survivor learns to forgive because he senses that his being unforgiving has blocked his life and held him back from healthier relationships. Not to forgive may have blocked him, too, from a closer relationship with a loving God.

Jesus' words helped me eventually to forgive the two people who had stolen my childhood. He said, "If you forgive those who sin against you, your heavenly Father will forgive you. But if you refuse to forgive others, your Father will not forgive your sins" (Matt. 6:14–15).

Some people teach that we don't need to forgive until the other person asks for forgiveness or acknowledges their wrongdoing. That's not true. Forgiveness doesn't depend on another's action. The person who was the victim forgives for himself.

Paul said it this way: "Get rid of all bitterness, rage, anger, harsh words, and slander, as well as all types of evil behavior. Instead, be kind to each other, tenderhearted, forgiving one another, just as God through Christ has forgiven you" (Eph. 4:31–32). Although Paul wrote to believers, nothing restricts our forgiving to only Christians.

Please note especially the last part: "Forgiving one another, just as God through Christ has forgiven you." The test of our understanding of and accepting divine grace is that we can forgive others because we know what it's like to be forgiven. At some point—and each adult survivor is different—he needs to forgive if he wants to live that joyful, abundant life that Jesus promises.

The victim's forgiving doesn't mean everything is wiped away as if it hadn't happened. Of course it happened, and forgiveness doesn't erase the past. But forgiveness enables him to stop living in the past, and keeps him from constantly reliving the pain.

The deep emotional pain goes away. That's certainly been true in my life. I went through a period of intense anger—even a short period of utter hatred, especially for my female abuser. Whenever her name came up in conversation or even in my thoughts, my stomach tightened, and sometimes I developed heartburn.

But now, years later, the pain is gone. I actually feel sorry for her and for the old man who abused me. They were victims of their own compulsive lust. They were addicted so badly that their needs and desires overrode my rights. I realize some may object to my use of the word addicted, but I believe it's accurate. Addiction refers to a compulsion, a need that controls a person's life. For me, this fits in that same category.

True forgiveness must also be a willing decision on the victim's part to no longer wish harm for the betrayer. Both of my perpetrators are dead, but even if they were alive, I wouldn't want them to have further pain or torment. If I forgive those who hurt me, no matter how deeply, I benefit. I can change. I become the winner. When we forgive, it puts the past into the past, and we don't have to live with it—and the pain—each day. To forgive allows us to admit that someone did something terrible to us but we have moved beyond the trauma.

To do that, we need God's help—and I had to cry out to God night after night for weeks to soften me and enable me to forgive. If we forgive, we become healthier, stronger, more human, and we place ourselves where we can freely receive God's grace.

What was done to the child was wrong, but the pain of the past no longer has to chain the adult survivor. Once he is able to forgive, it means he's no longer a victim. He is free. He can live joyfully in the present.

Some men don't reach that place. I believe to do so involves grace. It helped me to realize that I didn't deserve the grace in God's forgiveness. The more I perceive undeserved forgiveness from God, the more readily I can forgive those who hurt me.

Here's something that also worked for me, but it may not work for others. When Jesus hung on the cross, he prayed, "Father, forgive them, for they don't know what they are doing" (Luke 23:34). I don't try to absolve my abusers, but I do try to understand them and accept them as they are. I've forgiven them, but more than that, I understand they are sad, suffering human beings. Our perpetrators may deny their sins against us, but their denial doesn't mean they're not miserable, self-hating individuals.

My personal goal, then, was not only to forgive but to think of them with compassion. They don't know what they did. They don't realize the suffering they caused me because they were too blinded. My anger has slowly turned to compassion.

It has now been about fifteen years since I was able to forgive my perpetrators. If you asked me, I could reconstruct many of their acts. What I can't reconstruct—and don't want to anyway—is the pain or the anger. I can remember that I once had those feelings. The freedom from the emotional pain and the ability to talk freely about my abuse helps me to say, "Thank you, God, for healing me."

✦   ✦   ✦

One man I met years ago, in the now-defunct group called The Men's Experiment, said there are three steps a man has to take before he can forgive perpetrators:

1. Truth telling. The abused man must tell himself the truth about what happened. He must also tell at least one other person so that

it's no longer a secret. In telling the truth, he breaks the wall of secrecy that surrounds his abuse, and he purges himself of inner turmoil and the self-alienation that accompanies the abuse.

2. Accountability. That is, the victim must hold the perpetrator accountable for what he has done. This is true whether the survivor confronts the abuser or doesn't. Forgiveness begins to become possible once the man can say, "He molested me."

3. Refusal to let the perpetrator's evil deeds control the victim's thoughts. He can say, "He no longer has access to my emotions. I am free." When that happens, the victim is a step closer to being where Jesus wants him to be.

Some victims of abuse forgive more quickly than others. When he's ready, he'll be able to let go of the pain and no one will have to urge him to forgive. He will forgive because it's the obvious thing to do and because it's the right thing to do.

— 20 —

FORGIVING HIMSELF

How does a man who was abused forgive himself?

Does that sound like a strange question? *He* was the victim. That's true, and part of being the victim was that he probably accepted guilt that didn't belong to him. He was a child; he couldn't reason like an adult.

As a result, most adult survivors carry a great deal of guilt and perhaps even self-hatred. Here are a few typical statements a victim might make:

"I should have stopped him."

"I should have told on him."

"I should have hit him or screamed."

Joe talked about his self-hatred and how bad he must have been to deserve such treatment. "I felt as if God had abandoned me," he said. "My pastor abused me." If he couldn't trust God, how could he trust anyone? To Joe as a child, his pastor was like a stand-in for God, and the child wasn't mature enough to understand the distinction.

Others who were abused by clergy or prominent people in the community speak of not being believed when they tried to speak up. How could a victim find safety when he felt that everyone was aligned against him? That usually takes him to the next step: *I must be bad. Something must be wrong with me.*

Yes, he may need to forgive himself. He may need to forgive himself for having the grandiose belief that he should be an omnipotent, all-wise individual.

✦ ✦ ✦

The following is purely a personal observation, but those who have spoken to me of abuse by clergy told me of their deep spiritual hunger as children. They came to church leaders when they were spiritually open, hungry, and obedient children. They wanted to follow God. That spiritual sensitivity seemed to make them easy prey for so-called religious leaders—and it happens in all religions.

I've met men whose faith was destroyed by an abusive pastor. Some of them never come back to God. Others come back slowly.

If a man believes he is so damaged and unfit that even God wouldn't want him, that's a big battle to fight. My abusers weren't church leaders, but I understand that feeling. For a long, long time I was certain something was wrong with me. It's a common perception among the abused. If the survivor thinks he's at fault, as I did and as many others do, it's not easy for him to move past that. It is not, however, impossible.

Telling His Story in a Safe Place

One thing I think is absolutely true: when the abused are in a place of safety—most of us use the term "safe place"—we can face our pain and forgive ourselves. A safe place is where an individual or a group listens to what we need to say about ourselves. They believe us—because they understand our pain.

I'm convinced that telling his story is one of the major steps in an adult survivor's recovery. But the listener has to be someone who is supportive, who encourages him to press on past the pain, who loves him, and who has already established a trusting relationship with him. Simply telling his story may sound easy, but for many men that's difficult. When he learns he can trust another person, he's ready to reveal his experiences and to begin his healing journey.

He needs someone to listen without directing him. He needs to speak without being interrupted, questioned skeptically, or battling arguments.

As he feels stronger, he needs to widen his circle of trust and intimacy. It's a good idea for him to pray about talking to others he can trust. There are self-help groups in most cities, usually built on the Alcoholics Anonymous principle. I'm always quick to recommend Christians in Recovery and Celebrate Recovery groups. There are also a number of on-line groups to which he can safely and anonymously respond.

Whenever he speaks to anyone about his abuse and the information is held in confidence, it's easier for him to open up even more. Each time he feels safe with another person, he is steps farther down the healing path.

Listening to Others' Stories

A vital element of a man's being involved in a group of survivors of sexual assault is that he will hear others tell their stories. That's when he realizes, on an *emotional level*, that he isn't the only one. He realizes that the feelings he's carried with him for many years—the numbness, isolation, and guilt—aren't evidence that he is an evil man. He had a traumatic experience that deeply affects him, as it would any normal person.

Someone said it this way: "If the survivor of a shipwreck couldn't do anything but cling to a piece of driftwood, who would blame him for not trying to swim to shore? *He held on.* That was the best he could do."

Holding on is a good starting place. He did whatever he could to survive. When he meets other worthwhile, lovable people who once spent a significant amount of time and energy clinging to flimsy supports, they give him perspective on his own situation. Their victory gives him hope. "We made it. You can make it too." They have changed; they have found healing. He can too. Whenever any abused man takes charge of his life and shares his story with others, he proclaims the reality of recovery. With God all things are possible (see Luke 1:37).

A group setting of like-minded men can be a safe place. He won't have to attempt an explanation of why he feels as he does. He won't have to tell them why he did certain things. He can connect with other men without exposing himself to the risk of being abused. He's free to explore his feelings with others.

If he does choose to become part of a group, even though it's safe it won't always be comfortable. He spent a long time trying to avoid the pain. He probably stayed away from anything that reminded him of his stolen childhood.

Earlier I mentioned the group of six men with whom I met weekly for four years. I almost dropped out in the middle of the second year. I told myself I was healed and didn't need them. But I decided to hold on. During our first meetings we all agreed to follow one rule about leaving: if anyone felt it was time to drop out, he would tell us and come back the next week to "finish any old business."

As I pondered the matter of leaving, I realized the issue wasn't my being healed. I wanted to leave because I was scared. Those five men knew some of my deepest secrets. They had penetrated my defenses. I felt exposed and helpless. The easiest way out was to run away. I'm sure that realization came from outside myself, because the minds of survivors don't always let us see reality that clearly.

By deciding to stay one more week before I gave my notice, things changed. I felt accepted by the others—accepted on a deeper level than ever. Perhaps some inner part of me knew I was on the brink of fuller acceptance—and that frightened me.

I stayed four years until we moved out of state. By then, true healing had taken place. I had forgiven myself for my imagined guilt and for not being perfect. I was able to say that, as a child, I thought like a child and reasoned like a child. That empowered me to continue in my search for total healing.

✦   ✦   ✦

During the third year of my recovery, I read in the newspaper that the State of Georgia would sponsor a yearlong group of men who had been sexually assaulted in childhood. The group would meet in Atlanta, which is where I lived, and it would be free.

Before I called, I struggled with the decision because I'd begun to talk about my abuse and felt I had started down the healing path. But I finally called the number in the newspaper, and two psychologists who specialized in sexual abuse set up an appointment for me.

During the interview, I told them my story and what I had done in my own recovery. I told them I hadn't been able to trust myself to a therapist and that this had been a big hurdle for me.

"You don't need this group for your recovery," the lead therapist said, "but I think it can be helpful. You're probably further along than most of those who will join us."

That encouraged me and I signed up. At the first meeting we were fifteen men with a wide variety of experiences. The youngest was twenty and the oldest probably about fifty. The therapists asked each of us to give a brief history of our abuse. It wasn't comfortable for most of us. When some of them told their stories, tears came to my eyes. Two of the men in particular had horrendous stories of also being physically abused by their perpetrators. One man showed scars on his legs from cigarette burns.

Despite my discomfort, I stayed with the group. By the end of the year, however, only four of us remained. Two or three men stopped coming and we didn't know anything else. A few of them left messages on the therapists' answering machines. One man wrote a letter. Those who did notify us that they were leaving had what seemed like valid excuses, but the rest of us understood. One of the remnant said of someone who left us, "He's gone as far as he can. Maybe later."

"I hope they'll come back and try again with another group," another man said. He had been an alcoholic, and he told us it had taken him six attempts at sobriety before he finally made it, and he'd been alcohol free for three years.

The four of us who finished the course admitted it had been difficult. "I wanted to know who I am and I wanted to explore those things,"

Jack said, "but it hurts. I didn't know it would hurt so much to look into myself."

The group, though, didn't cause the pain. The group setting provided a safe place where we could *feel* our pain. We could express it, and by expressing it we could exorcise it.

One thing we refused to do—and it wasn't because of a rule, but because we each felt strongly about it—was to let anyone blame himself for the abuse. To my surprise, each of us tried to do that at some point during the year.

The group didn't heal me, but they supported me as I progressed. As far as I know, I was the only Christian in the group. The others allowed me to talk openly about my faith and how it aided me in my healing. For me, that was the test of the safety of the place. If I could talk about prayer and divine love and not be challenged, I knew I was in the right place.

As I've looked back over my group experience, it was good to have been with other men who felt the same inner pain that I had. For me, however, the loving encouragement from Shirley and David provided the foundation. And, of course, God was with me. God had been at my side during all the painful years, and that was the most important fact.

Connecting with the Inner Child

Here's something that helped me a great deal. A generation ago, Eric Berne developed a personality theory called Transactional Analysis, or TA, and it became quite popular. It was little more than a modernized version of Freud's theory, but Berne made it accessible to the average person and easy to work with. He said that all of us experience personal growth through a mixture of behavior, thought, and feelings. He defined three ego-states: (1) the parent—a parental, authority figure; (2) the adult—the mature part that lives in the present; (3) the child—when we revert to behaving similarly to the way we did in childhood.

Many have found TA useful. One friend said to me on several occasions, "You need to go back and love that child part of you. He's the one who was hurt because no one protected him."

That may seem bizarre to some, but he suggested I get quiet and talk to the little child inside me. "Assure him that you love him, are with him, and you'll protect him." Frankly, it did seem a bit strange to me, but I was open to trying almost anything. I did exactly as he suggested. I envisioned myself holding the five-year-old Cec, hugging him, and talking to him. As I did, I developed an immense sense of compassion for that long-forgotten part of myself. To my surprise, it was truly helpful for my healing. It's somewhat similar to seminars and workshops of a couple of decades ago. They taught people how to connect with their inner child, which is in the same vein as getting back in touch with the wounded parts of ourselves—our childhood.

If the adult survivor is able to access his pain, he can begin to heal. He can't undo the events of the past, but as he understands that little kid part of himself he can heal the still-open wounds. As he goes into the past, he doesn't have to search for every painful memory, worry about details or about total accuracy. He needs to interact with the *feelings* of the past, that is, to "stay on the feeling level."

When he returns to his little boy, it's a journey into pain. But, as an adult, as he enters into the past, he can bring healing with him. The adult may have to feel deep pain, regret, and sadness. He may relive many of the painful experiences of his childhood. But revisiting pain is part of the therapeutic process. As he opens the door to the pain, he also brings the cure with him.

As he acknowledges his lost childhood and talks to his little boy, he can mourn over what he didn't have and what he was entitled to have. He can connect with and push away the lies he heard and believed. In the process he can also feel the grief, the anger, and the outrage for being taken advantage of because he was small and naive.

He may have directed anger at himself for being weak or not fighting back, but his adult self can help the child to express anger toward the perpetrator. "He did this to me. He hurt me." As the adult and child direct their anger toward the perpetrator, that can lead to a determination to rise above the past. "We can recover; we will recover."

Abuse will no longer control his life. He can stand up to the molestation by taking charge and by embracing the hurting child. Instead of remaining in pain, he can evoke and experience it so that he can go through it and beyond it. He needs to say to the little boy in tender tones, "For a while we're going to have more pain, but this time we're stronger, and our recovery is the ultimate triumph over the man who abused you."

Recovery means he's taking charge of his life in a satisfying, adult manner. It means facing the reality of the pain, but allowing God's grace to work in his life. As he recovers, he can face the past and rise above it. He can feel positive about himself and establish healthy, adult relationships. Instead of staring at his failures and shortcomings, he can enjoy his strengths and talents.

As he recovers, he'll understand the past and use that awareness to create a healthier present and a stronger future for himself.

❖   ❖   ❖

Years ago, Tom, a friend in Louisville, wrote a letter to himself, forgiving himself. He wrote the things he did and didn't do to survive the abuse. He devoted one section of the letter to the things he had done to others because of his shame and deep-seated pain. One statement went something like this: "I didn't realize the negative things I was doing and how much I hurt those who were close to me. The more they tried to understand and love me, the more I pushed them away."

He also wrote, "I forgive myself for my rage. Because of Jesus' sacrifice, I know God has also forgiven me."

I like the way he forgave himself.

Other men have joined twelve-step programs. One element of those programs is that they encourage participants to make amends as a part of self-forgiveness for wrongs done.

✦   ✦   ✦

Once I forgave both of my abusers and myself, my life changed. To forgive myself was harder for me than to forgive them. My wife and a couple of my friends reminded me, "You're too hard on yourself."

Another friend helped me by saying, "If Cec Murphey were someone else and he asked you to forgive him, would you?" When I affirmed that I would, he laughed and said, "So what's the problem? Can't you be as kind to yourself as you are to others?" That interaction became a powerful moment of spiritual enlightenment. Yes, I could treat myself as kindly and as lovingly as I could friends, strangers, or perpetrators. If I had to point to a single experience in my recovery that stands out, it would be that moment.

"Cec, I forgive you." I must have repeated that sentence twenty times that day and kept saying it to myself for perhaps a week. Once or twice wasn't enough. It still took me that long before my own words penetrated and I could say, "Yes, I have forgiven myself."

It's very likely that most adult survivors have a similar problem. Like me, they may demand more of themselves than they would from others. They need to know that Jesus' command to love others as ourselves implies loving and accepting ourselves.

Jesus said it this way: "'You must love the LORD your God with all your heart, all your soul, and all your mind.' This is the first and greatest commandment. A second is equally important: 'Love your neighbor as yourself.' The entire law and all the demands of the prophets are based on these two commandments" (Matt. 22:37–40).

— *21* —

GOING PUBLIC

For adults who were abused as children, telling our stories can be powerful for us. It can be powerful for others, too, especially for those who haven't begun to talk about their traumatic past. They often have to cope with much shame and denial. To open up and shatter the silence of our past isn't easy, and some men never speak of it. They die with the secret buried deep inside.

Until I was able to talk openly about my abuse, I'd been haunted by the question: Will I ever be *normal?* I wondered if I would ever be acceptable to myself and to God. For many years I felt I wasn't worthy of God's love. Once I was able to stop thinking of myself as abnormal and unworthy (and it took a long time), I slowly accepted myself as worthwhile. I had moved from victim to survivor to victor.

If we tell our stories indiscriminately, though, we may find that not everyone is emotionally willing to listen. Instead of sympathy, our stories might elicit disgust. Some men have told the wrong people and have had regrets. Our victim-blaming society tends to protect offenders and scoff at victims. When I first mentioned the female relative who had abused me, I received several harsh, negative responses.

"No woman would do that to a child." (But they do.)

"How can a woman abuse a child?" (I could give you vivid details.)

"You must have done something to provoke it." (At ages two and three?)

One man laughed and said, "Wow, I wish a woman would abuse me." (He had no concept of rape or molestation.)

When we tell the wrong people, we risk setting ourselves up to be mistreated *again*. As adults, however, we have choices. We don't have to tell anyone. We don't have to tell, but if we find the right people at the appropriate time, it can be extremely liberating.

Some men have been more prudent about choosing whom and when to tell. The second therapist at our state-sponsored group said at our final meeting, "Tell it on a need-to-know basis. If you think it will make the relationship better or clear up problems, tell. Refuse to give information to people for whom it would have little meaning."

His words helped to guide me. It kept me from being indiscriminate in revealing myself. When I considered telling someone, I asked myself, *Will it help my recovery to speak up?* I couldn't always answer that one, but to ask the question forced me to reflect and to be cautious.

One thing I learned was to tell my story in small bits. In a conversation, if I mentioned I had been sexually abused, I tried to gauge the other's reaction. Sometimes there wasn't any apparent interest. Sometimes the person responded with something such as, "Oh, well, that's too bad. I'm sorry."

I'm able to accept those responses. It didn't shock them and they didn't seem to have bad opinions of me. When someone showed a serious, sympathetic interest, however, I sometimes told more. What I didn't want was a gossiper to spread stories everywhere, and I did have one minor experience like that.

The point of telling with discrimination is that it makes us feel less ashamed and less afraid. We sense we're on solid ground when we share. We may need to hold back details—especially in the beginning—because we don't want to overwhelm our listeners.

Public Announcements

In chapter 1, I mentioned the article I'd written about my abuse. It wasn't a face-to-face telling, but it was a big step for me. I've since written accounts for three different magazines. That article in *Light and Life* magazine was the first public step. I wanted to have my story out in the public because I decided that if it became common knowledge I wouldn't feel ashamed or guilty.

"It's time to stop feeling like a victim," I told my friend David Morgan. I wanted others to accept me as someone who had been deeply wounded and, by the grace of God, someone who also had been deeply healed.

The first time I spoke publicly about my abuse was on TV at Crossroads in the Toronto area, 100 Huntley Street. The host, Lorna Dueck, asked me if I would appear on her program, *Listen Up*, which was aimed at current issues. I did. The interview was supposed to last something like nine minutes. We went twice that long, so Lorna aired it as two segments.

No one contacted me as a result of that interview, but even so, it was a milestone for me. Once my story was "out there," it meant I had gone public. I had nothing to hide, and it gave me a good feeling to know that I had broken the silence.

Since 2004, I've spoken openly about my abuse. It gets easier each time. During the past few years, it's been easy to speak about my childhood. Tears no longer surface when I talk. But one of the best results is that people now contact me. From a writer friend I received an e-mail recently. She wanted to know if her husband could e-mail me or talk to me on the phone about his abuse. I answered yes, of course, to both. Two weeks went by before he called. "It took me that long to get up the courage," he said.

In 2008, I started a blog called Shattering the Silence to reach out to men (http://shatteringthesilence.wordpress.com). I printed postcards and displayed them at the table where I sold books. In Seattle, not many people picked them up, but Gary Roe did.

✦   ✦   ✦

Gary Roe's Story

As a result of early childhood abuse, I have struggled deeply with feelings of being alone. The abuse was revealed to me through a series of flashbacks over several years. It was a time of deep pain, confusion, grief, and anger.

In the midst of these flashbacks, I attended the annual Northwest Christian Writer's Association Conference in Seattle. I was walking through the conference bookstore, waiting for the first main session, when I noticed a postcard on the floor at my feet. I picked it up and read about an online ministry for male survivors of sexual abuse begun by Cecil Murphey. And Cec was the keynote speaker for the conference.

I stood there and stared at the postcard. I felt myself tearing up. I turned and walked outside, whipped out my cell phone, and called my wife, Sharon. I could hardly talk. Even though I was in counseling, and had shared with close friends and my congregation about my background, I still felt alone. One of the reasons I felt so alone was that I had yet to meet another man who had been through similar horrors (or at least, no man who admitted it). Now, this evening, I was going to meet a fellow male survivor.

That evening, after Cec spoke, I got in line to meet him. I had no idea what I was going to say. I tried rehearsing it repeatedly in my mind. When I got to him, all I could do was hold up the postcard. A sudden look of recognition passed across his face, and he hugged me. I felt myself tearing up again. He looked directly into my eyes and said something like, "I thank God for you. You're an answer to my prayers." (He had prayed to connect with other abuse victims.)

Over the next two days, Cec and I spent several hours together. Each moment was crucial for me. Here was someone who understood, who could relate, and who *knew*. As we shared our stories, I was blown away by the similarities of our experiences. I was also amazed that he could tell what I was thinking and feeling. I had found not only a brother, but a fellow soldier in this fight for freedom and healing. *He knew.*

Since then, every conversation I have had with Cec has been important to me. Yet I am still slow to reach out and initiate with him sometimes, even though I love him dearly. The shame and fear attached to
the abuse is great. The power of abuse lies in its secrecy. Every time I tell
my story, every time I call Cec, it is like coming out of hiding, and I feel
freer afterward.

My interactions with Cec actually led us to begin a ministry in our
church for survivors of sexual abuse and those who love us. It is called
Oasis. We must come out of hiding. We need each oth-er to heal and to
grow. By coming together, we begin to stand against this great evil. I am
far from alone.

*   *   *

Before He Goes Public

When and if the adult survivor is ready to tell his story, he needs
encouragement and support. But this significant fact must be kept in
mind: once he prints or broadcasts his story, he loses control over it.
People can tape the program and replay it. Just because it's a local show
doesn't mean it won't be sent elsewhere. If he tells his story in an open
public meeting, some of the participants may tell others. He will have
no power over how people respond. That's the risk, and he has to be prepared to take it.

I reasoned that nothing could hurt me as deeply as I had been hurt as
a child. I also reasoned that if I could be open about my abuse, including the use of my name, it would encourage others to speak up. I understand, though, those who choose to remain anonymous. That's why some
of the men in this book don't want to give their names, and I respect that
decision. One man told me, "I'm not a macho type." He mentioned other
things about himself. "In college, I took a lot of razzing because I didn't
sleep with girls. Some called me gay (which I'm not) and it hurt. I'm not
ready to be hurt again."

If he chooses not to reveal his name, that's fine. He has nothing of which to be ashamed. That's why I set up my blog the way I did. I wanted men to write without fear of being known.

He is entitled to this privacy—something he didn't have as a child. He has the right to choose those to whom he tells his story. When he was a child, he lived in a world of secrecy. He couldn't tell. Today he can, and he needs to understand that privacy and secrecy are not the same.

If he chooses to go public, he needs to be positive that abuse happened to him. He doesn't want someone, especially a relative or someone close to him, trying to talk him out of his experience or to minimize its effects. The accusation of bringing shame to the family can be a powerful tool against him.

In one instance the family disowned a son because of his "evil, spiteful ways." The son accused his father's employer of molestation. They were shocked and told the son, "It's a mean, horrible thing that you would make up such terrible stories." They told him he couldn't enter their house again until he stopped telling "those terrible lies."

When I heard the story, the man hadn't communicated with his family for about three years. At the time I thought, *Here's another victim who has been victimized again.* In his case, he refused to back down. "It happened. I can't deny what he did to me."

I admired him for his honesty, no matter what it cost him. Any victim who speaks out may pay a cost. I'd like every man to shout the abuse everywhere and get it into the open, but that's not realistic. If the survivor isn't prepared, if he begins to doubt his abuse or allows others to confuse him about what happened, he can be set back in his recovery.

Even after I'd received validation from siblings, at times doubt crowded in, especially concerning the female relative. I asked myself several times, *Did she really do that?* It was so painful, it might have been easier to say I imagined it. In fact, many times I hoped I would discover that I *had* only imagined it or that I'd succumbed to the false memory syndrome. But deep, deep inside, I knew the truth—or at least enough to keep moving forward.

The abuse was crime; it was sin. I was victimized as a child. I want to be clear on that. I'm thankful, though, for the outcomes. Because of what I've gone through in forging my way down the healing highway, I'm stronger. But I've received more than personal strength, I've learned compassion for others who hurt.

I don't praise God for the pain and the abuse. That would be insane. I thank God for grace and for the lessons I've learned through my own suffering.

— *22* —

POSITIVE EFFECTS

Here is one of the most amazing insights I had about myself: we give to others what we want for ourselves. I wanted love and protection, understanding and compassion. I didn't receive that as a child, but I reached out to others.

This morning, as I typed these words, I reflected on different periods of my life. I was the one who stood up for the underdog. I befriended several unpopular kids in school. One of them was Gene, a boy with a glass eye. Many kids shunned him because the glass eye didn't move.

As an adult, I taught sixth grade in the public schools for two years. Both years I asked for the kids who'd had the lowest achievement scores from the previous year. I expended a great deal of energy to teach them to read well. Each day I gave them word problems in math. Most of them scored grade level by the end of the year.

I can cite examples from our six years in Africa or my fourteen years as a pastor. They all make the same point: I felt a special connection to the lowly, the ignored, and the unloved. I offered them the qualities I'd wanted to receive myself.

When I became aware of that fact—only within the past few months before writing this—I saw it biblically as well. Jesus said, "Do to others whatever you would like them to do to you" (Matt. 7:12). I had quoted and repeated that verse many times, but it became a reality for me: I was following the golden rule. I reached out to others the way I yearned for someone to reach out to me. I gave what I wanted to receive. Perhaps that sounds simplistic, but it was a powerful realization to me. It helps me to understand that there was at least one positive aftereffect of my molestation.

These accounts demonstrate the truth of Romans 8:28—"We know that in all things God works for the good of those who love him, who have been called according to his purpose" (NIV)—and of 2 Corinthians 1:3–4: "the Father of compassion and the God of all comfort, who comforts us in all our troubles, so that we can comfort those in any trouble with the comfort we ourselves have received from God" (NIV). God can use all our experiences to make us better Christians, better people, better fathers, brothers, and friends.

My friend Patrick Borders says that negative experiences have helped him to understand people—their motivations, their desires. "I can see two sides to most stories. I can work as a peacemaker, or I can work to enlighten others by showing the truth that is buried in opposing views."

One man who was physically and sexually abused says, "Because of my pain, I've learned to reach out to others in their pain. Although I can get overly involved in others' struggles, I care, and I reach out to those who are hurting. I've learned to be someone who listens and will stand by others in times of trial. I've slowly learned that I can't solve their problems—that's God's business—although I still struggle with trying. I've found when I focus on listening, people have told me things they have never told anyone else. The hell I went through resulted in a unique understanding of suffering and an acceptance of other people's pain."

Another man says that he spent much time seeking answers by looking inward, and he had difficulty accepting himself. "I spent more time looking for the reasons than simply experiencing my life. As a Christian, the positive aspect is that I am contemplative. I've never been ambivalent about my faith. I am always reading. I am always seeking. I never take a break from trying to figure things out."

Those of us who have hurt and worked through our pain understand the hurts of others. We wish we could have had a different path, but this is the way it is. I've also learned that the more I reach out and help others, the stronger I become.

So mine is not purely an altruistic attitude, because I gain as well. I've been comforted. To use the current language, "I pay it forward" by comforting others. When we have moved past our pain and can feel the hurt of another person, that is a sign of true healing.

— 23 —

WHEN IS HEALING COMPLETE?

Is any man totally healed from childhood molestation? I don't know. I can speak for myself and say, "Not quite." I no longer feel the pain. Occasionally—and less frequently as time goes by—I have a flashback of an episode from my childhood. Even when I have one, it comes more like a memory of something that happened in the past with no heavy emotion tangled up with it. Despite that, I can sincerely say I've been healed, and for three reasons.

First, I can usually talk about my sexual abuse without tearing up. I don't feel strange or odd when talking about the experience. To the contrary, speaking about male sexual assault, and especially when I tell about my own, strengthens me.

Second—and some men never make this stage—I look back and thank God. I'm not thankful for the abuse, but I am thankful for the good things that have come out of my dealing with it.

Third, above I said, "not quite." While working on this book, I resisted writing. I put it off as much as I could until I realized I was resisting. For many writers, that's common; but it hadn't happened to me before. But then, I hadn't tried to write a book about sexual abuse before.

I pushed aside my desire not to write, and silenced my resistance. "I have to get this written," I said to myself several times. I asked others for prayer, and I pushed myself.

I finally finished. Completing the task of writing about my abuse and opening myself to others who might misunderstand or find my story revolting assured me that I had traveled a long way toward complete healing.

After I turned the manuscript over to my proofreader, I became aware that tension had built up during the writing. Only after I relaxed was I aware that I'd been tense. I hadn't felt any strong emotional reactions, but something deep inside me resisted writing the book. Perhaps I was afraid of old feelings returning. Perhaps I didn't want more pain, or maybe I didn't want to relive the past.

Shirley spotted the tension, even though she wisely said nothing until I brought it up. She'd been able to see it by the way I walked, and sensed it in our lovemaking. I, though, had been only vaguely aware. But, aware or not, the past hadn't completely disappeared. Maybe it will now. Perhaps writing this book will be my final step of healing.

Beyond my healing, I hope this book will aid you, my readers, as you try to help the men in your life who were once abused to stretch toward the end of the healing road.

— Part 2 —

HOW YOU CAN HELP HIM

THE OTHER VICTIM

You are the other victim. He was molested, shamed, taken advantage of, and deeply hurt. But his life and behavior since that time have affected you as well.

If he came to you with his story, you may have been shocked. But it's also true that he trusted you enough to confide in you. If he told you his story, that means he considers you a safe person. If he told you, it's because he wants your help.

What kind of responses can you give him? That's what the rest of part 2 is about. But here are a few suggestions for starters.

First, be honest in what you say. If you feel powerless—and you probably do—it's all right to say that. But even when you feel powerless, you can listen.

Second, you can't say anything that will make him feel better—and it wouldn't be helpful to try—but you can be a person to whom he can open his soul. Give him reason to trust you.

Third, if you're angry at the perpetrator or at a parent who "let it happen," it's understandable that you feel that way. But he doesn't need angry words or horrified responses. He needs a loving, compassionate listener. He may not speak these exact words, but this is what he's saying: *This is my life. This is what I live with. I want you to understand my pain.*

If the man you care for tells you his secret, you might say, "I don't understand all you've been through or how you must feel. But I love you, and I want to know, and I want to help you in any way I can." A simple statement like that might be enough. If he sees that you want what is best for him and have committed yourself to his healing, he can learn to trust you. Allow for his silences or mood shifts.

When I first opened up to Shirley she didn't understand how an adult could hurt a child that way, and she didn't realize all the emotional trauma of an adult survivor of childhood abuse. She was shocked and hurt for me, but she listened. I didn't expect her to understand everything else. How could she? She'd never been exposed to individuals who'd been abused.

Fourth, he needs you to believe him. "I'm so sorry that happened to you," tells him that you do believe him.

Fifth, he needs to know that you won't tell anyone without his permission. Confidentiality is important to him. If he suspects you'll tell your best friend or someone else, he might be afraid to open his heart to you. Perhaps you need to ask yourself, *Why should he trust me?* After all, someone he trusted betrayed him, so why wouldn't he expect the same treatment from you?

Sixth, this might be the first time he's ever talked openly. He might be embarrassed as well as ashamed. As an adult, he may have forgotten that it happened, or that he responded as a child would. Gently remind him, "You did the best you could." You may need to say, "You survived that awful time in your life." You may also remind him that he had to do it totally on his own. Most likely there was no one in whom he could confide or ask questions. "But you have me now. I won't laugh, and I won't ridicule you."

He may need to know that he was a courageous person. He lived through the abuse and didn't give up or harm himself. "Despite your pain and betrayal, you learned to cope."

Seventh, if he struggles with addictions—even the addiction of overeating—remind him that he *unconsciously* chose them as medication for his pain. By your compassionate acceptance, you can't free him from his addictions, but you can stay beside him while he fights. He has an ally in you—and you may be the first one he's ever had.

Eighth, you might be his best conduit to God. Probably he prayed many times in the past. He may have prayed for the abuse to stop. You don't have to explain or even attempt to explain why God didn't answer. Simply say, "I don't know," because you don't, "but I'm here for you now. I'm here to encourage you, to pray for you, and to pray to God on your behalf."

And pray for yourself, too. You didn't ask for this situation and had nothing to do with creating it. But you are affected by it anyway, and you will need God's help, too, as you help him.

✦   ✦   ✦

Throughout these chapters, I'm offering ideal responses. As the man in your life struggles through various aspects of dealing with his abuse, and as you learn more about what occurred in his childhood, you may not be able to handle such an emotional load on your own. If it's too demanding or draining for you, get help. Go to your pastor or see a professional who understand abuse issues.

If you want professional help, tell the man in your life what you plan to do. Explain that you want to support him as much as you can, and that if you get professional help, you can become more effective.

With most survivors, trust is an extremely significant issue. Assure the man in your life that you won't betray his secrets. "I want professional help because of my needs. I want to stand by your side and go through the painful process with you, but I can't do it alone." Ask him to tell you how much he's willing to let you reveal to a professional. You may need to promise that you won't violate his trust.

As a significant woman in his life, you are important. He needs you. You might be able to help him to heal his wounds when no one else can.

25

ACCEPT HIS UNSPEAKABLE PROBLEM

During his childhood, in many of his relationships the love was *conditional*. If he was the good boy or if he cooperated, he was rewarded; if not, love was withheld. As an adult, his trust level might be low; he may fear betrayal by another significant person in his life. *Unconditional* love requires your commitment to listen to and to accept him even if you don't understand the things he says or does.

This book is meant to help you understand his behavior, though, not fix it. It's unfortunate that many women believe that if they love their men enough they can fix them. They believe that if they find exactly the right thing to say, everything will be all right. Your words, though, won't heal; your absolute commitment to him may.

Elsewhere I've mentioned the group of six men who gathered together every Thursday night for four years. In our first meeting, each of us answered a question: "What do you want to get out of this group?"

I was first and said, "I want intimacy with men above the waist."

They knew exactly what I meant. For many abused men, it's difficult to distinguish between love and eroticism. An embrace should be just an embrace, but for many men who were once abused, it's not so simple. In our childhoods, a tender touch from a male led to sexual behavior.

To compound the problem, many men have trouble discussing their masculinity. As a result of childhood abuse, lurking deep inside them might be the gnawing fear that he's not a real man or that he may secretly be a homosexual. In relationships with other men, he may secretly fear that his affection for another is actually erotic desire. In chapter 13, I write about men who cover up those fears by acting like a super macho stud.

The childhood of the man you care for was destroyed by a selfish predator. Although he knows he's heterosexual, he may have doubts. Or he might be afraid that others will think there's something wrong with him. Now that you understand why he behaves that way, you can be sensitive to that unspoken problem and realize anything that threatens his maleness renews his fears. He might, for example, be afraid to express any affection in words or gestures toward another man. To do so may indicate, if only to himself, that something is wrong with him. So avoid urging him to have physical contact with another male if he's clearly uncomfortable in doing so.

Here are two words you're going to see a lot. *Be patient.* Accept him as he is, and help him accept that his fears are simply his current reality. When his fears are eased, his reality can change.

26

BELIEVE HIM AND HELP HIM BELIEVE

If you want to be part of his healing, you need to be aware of your own attitudes and emotions. After you learn of his experience, monitor your feelings: Are you becoming intolerant or doubt his sexual assault? If you continue to ask him, "Do you think that really happened?" he will likely retreat. Not only does he have to face his own doubts but he will have to combat yours as well.

A man who was sexually assaulted needs someone to believe him. He may have had experiences with people who didn't believe him or whom he felt wouldn't believe him.

It's understandable that you may have questions about the abuse, but for the time being, focus on his needs. This is his problem. Stay emotionally available to him and be a source of positive support. Whatever negative feelings you express about his abuse can make him feel that he is less of a man.

If he is to achieve total healing, he must be believed. Listen and remain open to listening. Avoid questioning details or contradictions. You might be the first person to whom he has opened his heart, and if you focus on clarifying, especially in the beginning, he may interpret that as unbelief, doubt, and skepticism from you. He needs your encouragement to help him face the reality of his past. He not only needs to be believed, but also encouraged.

If you show your outrage at his story of abuse by saying something like, "I can't believe anyone would do such a thing to a child!" you might do a great deal of harm to his healing. Imagine what it must be like to tell someone that something horrible happened to you, and not be believed. It happens, and may have happened in the past to the man you care for. If so, can you imagine the pain he must now be going through? Not only was he victimized by the abuser, but he's victimized a second time because others don't believe him. Or imagine what it must be like *never* to have told anyone because you think no one will believe you. Not being believed is the second trauma of abuse.

You don't want to add to his pain. You care about this man, and you can sense the hurt he endures. So if you have doubts, leave them unspoken. Avoid statements like, "Maybe you're mistaken or confused about what happened." Or worse, "I'm sure you're wrong about so and so. Are you sure he did that?" Granted, some of his revelations may be so revolting it's hard to believe that an adult could so abuse a child. Be prepared. *Don't let him down when he talks to you.*

Among the group of fifteen men who started together in the state-sponsored program was the tendency to minimize the abuse. All of us admitted it happened, but several brought up mitigating circumstances:

"I was lonely."

"I needed affection."

"I deserved what I got."

"Yes, it hurt but I've gotten past it."

These statements indicate that the victim himself is having a hard time fully believing that abuse took place. They are not the statements of emotionally healthy men. But when men are heard and believed, they can respond in healthy ways. One man, whose first name was Ben, cried for several minutes after he told his story. "You believe me!" he yelled, "You believe me!" He must have said that five or six times. He hugged us and thanked us. Although he never came back, I think we became a milestone in his recovery.

✦   ✦   ✦

You can't help him reinvent or change his childhood, but you can help him overcome the pain from that period. You can help him *believe* that he can overcome the pain. As he feels significant, wanted, and valued, he has the emotional tools to go beyond his loss of childhood.

As I urge in a number of places in this book, listen to him. Encourage him to feel sad or angry—whatever he needs to feel. If he throws out his anger and you don't recoil, he begins to believe that he can trust you, and you have become an instrument of healing.

His childhood was stolen and he can never recover it, but you can help him understand what happened. Many abuse survivors unconsciously try to undo the past. It's as if they think that going back to what happened will change it. It's not logical but purely emotional. They still live in the past and need help to move into the present. They need to embrace the hurting child inside themselves and to love him. They need to believe that child deserves to be loved. Too often they look down on that child for being weak or imperfect, and they accuse themselves for not being stronger or able to fend off the abuse.

Remember this and remind him: *His childhood was stolen and he can never, never recover it.* Although he can't recover the past, what he can do—and this is where he needs your help—is to recover from the *loss.* And he needs to believe that he *can* recover from it. As he believes more strongly that he is significant to you, every time you show him compassion, you are putting salve on his wounds.

He needs to believe in you, that he can trust you, even if he's not aware of that need. Be patient. He's been given lots of conflicting messages and little true love.

✦   ✦   ✦

When my memories began to return, they hurt. The pain overwhelmed me at times. But another part of my mind whispered, "This isn't true. You're making this up." Until I spoke with other survivors of sexual abuse, I assumed that whisper was unique. I've learned that it's common among those of us who lived in denial or who had amnesia as a result of the overwhelming pain.

When abuse survivors strive to recapture the memories, at some point we begin to doubt. We wonder if we're only making it up. *Maybe I wanted sympathy. Maybe I really wanted Shirley to think it was worse than it was.*

Or maybe I was afraid to believe the truth about my childhood.

For me, the break came when I talked to one sister, who had also been abused by the old man. She confirmed several things, and another sister confirmed facts about the female relative. I spoke to my two younger brothers. Although neither directly admitted the abuse, they did make sideways allusions to it, and it was obvious that they weren't able to cope with the memories. Even so, their reactions confirmed several things for me.

The man in your life might be like the person I was. Maybe he needs someone to believe him and to encourage him when he struggles with denial of the truth. Maybe he needs *you*.

In the beginning you might be shocked to hear his story. Please listen anyway. He needs to confide and to open up. Part of him may want to say, "This is all made up." But the pain reminds him it's true.

Believe him and that will help him believe.

27

SUPPORT HIS SPIRITUAL RECOVERY

God is a loving father. It's the most common way to speak about God in the church. But for many adult survivors, that's one of the most difficult aspects of God to identify with. This is especially true if shame remains an issue in our lives and we feel unlovable.

My father was an alcoholic and sometimes brutal. Not once in my childhood did I ever sense he loved me. Some men were sexually assaulted by their fathers. How can we possibly relate to the loving fatherhood of God? Shame, too, makes us feel unworthy and interferes with our following a loving, accepting God.

I became a believer as an adult. For me one significant change came when I attended a church where the minister referred to God as a loving father. I didn't have a church background, and the only god I remembered hearing about was the so-called peeping Tom who constantly watched for me to do something bad so he could swoop down and punish me.

Although I had no earthly role model of a loving father, when I heard about a loving Father, those words touched me. I didn't understand what the words meant, but something inside me yearned to know such a father. It took me years to realize how much of a loving, accepting parent God is. But all along I knew what I wanted.

If you grew up with a loving father, you—as the woman in an adult survivor's life—may be able to help him recognize the attributes of such a man. What does having a loving father mean to you? How did your earthly father show his love to you? How did he show care and concern for others? You could talk about those things and ask the man you care about if he knows a man who shows those characteristics. Even if you didn't have a warm, loving father, you can encourage him to develop a relationship with another man who can show him those attributes. Tell him that you'll pray for him to find such a man, and encourage him to pray, if he can, for God to place a man like that in his path.

Perhaps, too, you can guide him through and out of his feelings of being unworthy of such a father. Using your own experience, help him understand that God *desires* to become *his* loving father.

The man you care for needs your affirming presence so he can embrace the spiritual aspect of recovery. And he needs your support. Shirley didn't talk much about God's love for me, but she demonstrated it, and I saw God's love through her unrelenting commitment to my spiritual recovery. Shirley was at my side as I took each tentative step forward. When I wanted to pull back, she whispered, "You can do it." And I did. You, too, can help the man in your life.

One of the most helpful things to me as a Christian was reading about God's love in the Bible. It wasn't easy for me to acknowledge that I'm lovable simply because God created me and, as they said a generation ago, "God don't make no junk" and "God don't make ugly."

I also discovered renewal by being in church with other worshipers around me. Something about the corporate singing and praying touched me and enabled me to feel part of worship as I hadn't before. It seemed I was able to transcend my personal issues while I was in that atmosphere.

I found much help, too, during the ten years I participated in groups outside the organized church. I received immense help and encouragement from them, for which I'm truly grateful. Mutual-help groups outside the church are seriously lacking, though, in that while they can point us to God or a higher power, they don't address our need for Jesus Christ. I didn't leave the church during that period, but I often put more energy into those groups than I did in serving and worshiping. After ten years of working with men's groups, I finally left. To serve some vague higher power wasn't enough for me.

For that stage of my spiritual development, though, I needed the support of men who would allow me to express my deepest feelings and inmost thoughts. I couldn't find that in the church. That's changed. A number of Christian recovery groups have come into existence. Celebrate Recovery, for example, is one such group, and I've spoken a number of times at their meetings. The first time I spoke at one, in Loma Rica, California, I said, "I've found my tribe." I understood those people and I connected. They came because of a plethora of issues, but all of them were in recovery of some kind and moving toward healing.

In the mid-90s, according to their Web site, www.celebraterecovery .com, Saddleback Church in Lake Forest, California, launched Celebrate Recovery with forty-three people. The program was designed to help those struggling with hurts, habits and hang-ups by showing them the loving power of Jesus Christ through a recovery process. Celebrate Recovery has helped more than ten thousand people at Saddleback, attracting over 70 percent of its members from outside the church. Eighty-five percent of the people who go through the program stay with the church and nearly half serve as church volunteers.

You may need to remind the man in your life that God loves him and has promised to give him the strength he needs. The more you can embody compassion and understanding, the more those qualities can point him to a loving, caring God.

28

HELP HIM HONOR HIS BODY

I had read a great deal about females who have been sexually assaulted before I discovered books about males. I also realized there are many similarities in the issues of those who have been abused, both male and female. The one that struck me most is the lack of understanding regarding our own bodies.

Many times the legacy of childhood abuse can show up in unrelated ways, such as in an eating disorder. Sometimes those who have been abused cope by "medicating" themselves through food.

I finally understood that in my own life. For many years I had no accurate perception of my body. I believed I weighed too much. I looked at myself in the mirror but I didn't see my true image. I'm 5 feet, 7 inches and weigh almost 140 pounds. That's thin. But for years I couldn't see myself as thin. I knew I wasn't fat, but I assumed I needed to weigh less.

The abused man in your life may likely have some distorted idea about his body. Some men become preoccupied with their bodies. It may start because they believe they are ugly or at least unattractive. When they view themselves in a mirror they see only a hideous or unsightly body. Others, of course, go to the opposite extreme and assume that their bodies are the only thing that gives them value. If they have muscular bodies, they assume people will like them. They constantly compare their physique to others to see if they are the most physically attractive in the room. Being called a hunk, or something similar, is what they yearn to hear. In their minds, they *are* their bodies.

I also know men who ignore their bodies. They don't seem to care about the way they look or how they dress. It's almost as if they dissociate from their bodies.

The point is, sexual abuse creates mental, spiritual, emotional, as well as physical issues. So the effects of abuse may show up in his body.

A full recovery involves all the areas of life. But he needs your help to achieve it. If you sense he has issues with body image, ask him about it and let him tell you. "I understand that you may have issues with body image. How do you perceive your body?" His perception of it may come out sounding strange, but when he looks into a mirror, that's how *he* sees himself. If he sees himself as thinner or fatter than he is, you needn't try to convince him otherwise. Logic or argument won't change his self-assessment, anyway. For now, accept his self-misperception as a symptom of his molestation.

It may encourage you to know that confused body images are typical symptoms of men who were sexually molested. So here's my suggestion. Softly and kindly, help him accept himself. Rather than focus on his mistaken perception of his body image, focus instead on assuring him of your commitment to him.

I don't know how much Shirley grasped about the way I perceived my body. At the time, I wasn't even aware that I had a misperception. I know it now. Just to type this sounds strange, but it's true. Only after I had traveled the road to healing for a long time was I able to look at myself in a mirror and see what I really looked like. The distortion is gone, and that gives me stronger assurance that I've experienced recovery.

When I struggled over issues involving my body, a few significant verses helped me to see that my body belongs to God. Here are two of them:

> Don't you realize that your body is the temple of the Holy Spirit, who lives in you and was given to you by God? You do not belong to yourself, for God bought you with a high price. So you must honor God with your body. (1 Corinthians 6:19–20)

I plead with you to give your bodies to God because of all he has done for you. Let them be a living and holy sacrifice—the kind he will find acceptable. (Romans 12:1)

You can help the man you care for with gentle, very gentle, reminders that his body belongs to God. God created his body, and everything God created is good.

✦   ✦   ✦

I heartily recommend exercise—in whatever form that works for him. If he already exercises, encourage him to continue. If he doesn't exercise, *telling* him to do so is probably not the best approach. But you might say, "I understand that exercise can help you feel better mentally and physically. Do you think taking a walk every day might be beneficial for you?" If you're able, you might offer to join him.

Intense, aerobic exercise often triggers memories. It was true in my case. Running played a significant role in my recovery, and helped me get in touch with my body. From my experience, and that of others, I suggest finding a repetitive form of exercise that keeps the body moving without concentration. Running or fast-paced walking are excellent.

Physical exercise is good for everyone, and the benefits are multiple. It strengthens muscle groups, lowers blood pressure, and helps with weight control. But it also improves mood. Physical activity is helpful to those who struggle with depression. Years ago I learned that any aerobic exercise releases the endorphins that elevate our mood and lower our stress levels. Experts recommend getting a go-ahead from the doctor, and to start out slowly, then work up to some form of vigorous exercise at least three times a week for half an hour or longer.

Although I've run for thirty years, at first I didn't realize that when I dashed down the streets, I could also meditate. I learned to create a mental space that cleared my mind and pushed away negative thinking.

An additional benefit of exercise is that it enhances a sense of self-esteem through realizing what we can accomplish.

One of my friends said, "When I run, it gets me out of my head and I feel connected to my body." That may be the message the man in your life needs from physical activity. The more he gets in touch with his body, the more he perceives it clearly and the more he honors it. You can encourage him to do that.

29

ACCEPT HIS SHAME

For most victims of abuse, shame has been part of our identities. If we don't deal with shame, we don't outgrow it and it doesn't disappear. Our feelings of shame might be difficult for us to identify and explain, but they're real and they're powerful. No amount of insight or logic heals shame. Our shame came from an abusive relationship—when someone else made us feel worthless or bad. We felt we were not loved—couldn't be loved.

One man I remember only as Rolf had been abused as a child and now, at age thirty-one, he almost became victimized again. He'd been to a concert and had missed the last bus home. Another man offered him a ride and he accepted. In the car, the man put his hand on Rolf's left leg.

"Don't, please," Rolf said. But he heard the voice of a child coming out. The man laughed and said, "I won't hurt you."

"His words sounded like the perp in my neighborhood. I knocked his arm away and demanded that he stop the car." Rolf had to walk more than three miles, "But it was worth it."

We applauded him. Even though it had been twenty-two years since his molestation, the wounded boy was still inside.

"As I walked home, a strong sense of shame came over me," Rolf said. "I kept beating up on myself for being trapped by a perp." He got out of the situation, but the shame had stayed with him.

The men in our group helped Rolf because we congratulated him on doing the right thing. Talking to others he can trust can help the man in your life. As part of his healing, encourage him to open up to other men. One advantage of being part of any mutual-help group is that feeling of acceptance. He can get a reality check on himself and his relationships, and about issues related to shame. He can talk about these things to other survivors that he couldn't mention to friends and co-workers. If he resists the idea, ask him if he will at least pray, and tell him that you will pray about it too.

The man you care for may struggle with the ignominy, regardless of how long ago the assault took place. You can't replace his loss of self-respect, and your denying his feelings—"You shouldn't feel that way"—can only increase the loss. You're not his therapist, but if you can listen without directing him, you've already helped him immensely.

Acceptance and the Inner Child

In regard to dealing with his shame, if the process below seems workable, please encourage the abused man in your life to try the technique. Encourage him not to worry about total accuracy, but to "stay on the feeling level."

Ask him to address the little boy he was. Encourage him to tell the inner child that he wasn't bad, but what was done to him was bad.

Here are some things you can urge him to say:

"You did the best you could."

"You faced situations no child should have to encounter."

"You didn't understand what was done to you."

"I love you. You're not alone."

"Together we'll heal the wounds."

"You were hurt and you suffered, but you survived the abuse. Together we'll receive healing."

"God gives us power and inner strength. God will help us heal."

"You were a child. You felt helpless—and you were. But now you have me. Together we have the Lord to get us through this."

Be the person who accepts him in the condition he's in right now. The more accepting you are of his deep, inner feelings, the more your attitude encourages him to accept himself. One day he may be able to say, "What I did was the best I could do at that level of immaturity."

Pain and Healing

During my recovery, I grasped an important fact: recovery is not solely about the lessons we learn; even more, it's learning to feel that heals us. It's like the doctor who treats an illness and says, "This will hurt." We have to experience the pain before we get rid of it.

Emotions associated with his abuse recovery might be powerful. At times he may wonder how he could hurt so badly. He can't *think* his way into recovery and he can't command recovery of himself. The experts agree that the experience of selfless love and acceptance from at least one other person is necessary for his recovery. Here's where he needs the acceptance of a loving woman. Here is where he needs you.

In the words of John, "We love each other because he loved us first" (1 John 4:19). The principle is that once we experience love from others, we are enabled to love. To get rid of his shame, he has to feel accepted for being who he is.

You need not take on the burden of trying to carry all his emotional baggage. You can't anyway. But be available to listen, to express your love, and to strengthen him when he grows weary or belittles himself. Be the safe person from whom he doesn't need to hide his self-mortification.

Sex and Intimacy

I want to mention sex here because that's where the abuse started and that's where his feelings of shame originate. Some men have immense difficulty discussing their feelings about sex. Most of us carry around mental images of "real men" and their exciting sexual lives. I doubt that any man lives up to the stories portrayed in books and films.

Some survivors fear intimacy—which goes far beyond sex. It's difficult for them to have a meaningful sexual relationship because true intimacy involves being vulnerable, emotionally and spiritually sharing one's most personal self, and sharing one's body. Vulnerability reminds him of being taken advantage of as a child; his emotional and spiritual self may not be healed enough to share with you; he's reminded that, as a child, his body was taken from him. He didn't give consent: he didn't know how.

If you are his wife, his shame and his pain contribute to his inability to be truly intimate, and that can affect your ability to be intimate. Because each man is different, I can't offer you any cure-all to heal him. Again, be patient. Let him understand true intimacy slowly and thus more meaningfully.

— *30* —

REMIND HIM THAT YOU CARE

Here's one of the best ways to remind the man you care for that you do, indeed, care: treat him so that he feels worthwhile. You may need to help him believe he's not damaged goods, and you might say that to him in several ways: "You're not a freak"; "You didn't deserve what happened to you."

You may need to say such words to him often because he has believed lies. Maybe he believed it was his fault, that he's not lovable, and that he can't ever live a normal life. When he doubts himself and when he repeats the lies he has believed about himself, you can help him by repeating the truth to him.

At one particularly difficult time in my recovery, I was ready to confess to my friend David what I considered the deepest, darkest secret of my abuse. It was so painful I hadn't been able to tell anyone.

As I told Dave Morgan, I watched for the slightest sign of unbelief or disgust. I saw none. I continued and finally finished.

"And?" A puzzled look came into his eyes.

"What do you mean?" I asked.

"And what else?"

"That's it," I said.

"Oh."

That response was exactly what I needed. I had expected to shock him. I wondered if he would (in a nice way) begin to distance himself from me.

From his simple, one word, "Oh," I knew I could trust my friend with anything. He demonstrated what each of us needs: compassion and understanding when we can't understand or feel kindly toward ourselves.

As I mentioned earlier, a few years ago in Louisville I joined a group of men who met on Saturday mornings. I liked them and enjoyed being with them. I worked from home and rarely saw anyone during the day, so I occasionally invited one of the men to have lunch with me at a local restaurant. All of us were wounded in some way; all of us were on the healing journey. Some had been sexually abused. A few spoke of extreme physical abuse; some of sexual, physical, and verbal battering.

One Tuesday, I invited Louie to lunch. It lasted about an hour. He told me his story, which was sad. Louie was about four inches over six feet, muscular, and in his late thirties, but he believed himself to be "a worthless wimp."

After lunch I hugged him in the parking lot and thanked him for having lunch with me. We both drove away.

The following Saturday Louie spoke up to the group and mentioned that he and I had been to lunch. "I kept waiting to find out what he wanted from me," Louie said. He spoke of the good conversation and the relaxing time. "When we left the restaurant together, I thought, okay, now he'll tell me what he really wants."

Louie laughed before he said, "He hugged me, said goodbye, and drove away." Just then the smile left, replaced by tear-filled eyes. "I'd never had anybody do that before. They always wanted something. Cec didn't want anything from me."

I did want something: I wanted his friendship. I needed healthy relationships with other men. Louie and I never became close friends, but we had a solid relationship. I moved a few months later so we lost contact, but I cared about him and he understood that. He also cared about me, and I understand that.

When I attended my last Saturday meeting because Shirley and I had decided to return to Atlanta, the guys had a special going-away party. A time came for men to speak words of appreciation, and Louie was the first to speak. "Cec is the first man who ever showed me he liked me for who I am and not for something I could do for him."

That time tears filled my eyes.

✦ ✦ ✦

Caring and showing compassion is a central message in this book. I've mentioned a few suggestions for things to do or say, but nothing will be more helpful to his healing than for you to express your loving concern. If he knows you're with him and want him healed, you can make his struggles easier.

He'll know that someone else stands beside him. That might feel strange to him, and he may test you. He may watch for ways you might take advantage of him, or he may reveal information that is particularly disturbing or shocking just to see how you accept it.

Why wouldn't he test you? When he was victimized, someone he trusted, perhaps even loved, took advantage of him. If he tests you, accept it as part of his growth. "Nothing you can say or do," you might say, "will keep me from loving you." He needs to prove to himself that your compassion is genuine.

Sexual assault influenced every part of his life. His communication style, his self-confidence, and his trust levels have been affected. He already has feelings of worthlessness. He may feel, as I did, that he isn't a whole person—that part of him is missing. Let him be who he is right now, and hold his hand as he moves forward. Let him deal with his own issues. You can't heal the pain for him, but you can stand by him as he becomes healthier. *You can become his cheerleader.*

Though you can't heal him, I urge you not to ignore or minimize his pain. Think of his brokenness as an open wound. No matter what advice and medication he receives, the body must heal its own wounds.

So what can you do?

Say, "I love you. I'm here whenever you need me."

Those two sincerely spoken sentences may be exactly what he needs.

31

LISTEN, LISTEN, LISTEN

Listen—but only when he's able to talk. Don't push. As a victim, he was forced, coerced, manipulated, and cajoled, so avoid urging him to lay bare his soul. He needs to open up on his own terms. Give him time, space, and assurance that you're there to listen when he needs to talk.

Too few people realize the importance of what I call active listening, which we'll talk about later in this chapter. Basically, it's setting aside whatever time it takes for him to talk. He may need to tell parts of the story several times. Let him.

I have a theory about that. For some of us, the pain has seared our hearts so deeply that it's not enough for us to tell an account once. Maybe even three times isn't enough. In the early days of my recovery, I realized that I repeated things I'd said before. One time when I spoke to David Morgan I stopped and apologized. "You've heard this before."

"But you need to say it again," he said.

A simple sentence like that gave me permission to tell a story as often as I needed. I'm not aware that the telling became easier each time. I am aware that after repeating an incident several times, I no longer needed to talk about it. There must have been dark corners of the story that I hadn't coped with and I needed to bring the entire account into the light over several tellings. Only by doing that could I overcome the pain.

Supportive Silence

Silence, too, can be a powerful healing tool—when it's the right kind of silence. Most adult survivors, though, are afraid of silence. We're uncomfortable with it. We need noise around us all the time. If we have outward noises, we don't have to turn inward.

One of the powerful moments in my healing came after I'd watched a TV special on sexual molestation. I remember only that it was a Canadian woman who told her story. I was in shock as I listened to her tell not only of the abuse but of the ways in which she coped.

When the program finished, I couldn't talk. "I need to go for a walk," I told my wife and left the house. I walked for about an hour. I came back and sat on the front steps. So many powerful emotions surged through me, I didn't know how to express what was going on and, at the time, I couldn't even pray clearly. The woman's story, although different, resembled mine in many ways. The TV special stirred memories faster than I could sort them out.

When I went inside, Shirley had already gone to bed. I crept into the room, still dressed, and quietly got into bed. She turned over and put her arms around me. She didn't say a word, but she held me.

I felt safe. As I lay in her arms, I knew everything was all right—my wrestling with my emotions, my inability to express them, my need to walk and be silent. She accepted my need for all that. I didn't have any great moment of insight; I didn't cry. I relaxed, and the tormenting confusion slowly dissipated and I fell asleep.

When I awakened the next morning, I felt lighter in heart than I had for months. I was able to pray and talk to God about some of the issues the program raised. I sensed I had passed some kind of mark in my growth.

If Shirley had tried to talk to me the previous night, or tried to get me to talk to her, I would have shut down. She honored my silence. I tell this account to encourage you not to be afraid to sit with no words between you.

On another occasion, I hurt badly but didn't know how to talk about it with my friend David. I stopped and stared into space, trying to find words to explain my feelings. David laid his hand on mine. Just that simple gesture. He was there; I was aware of his presence, but it wasn't intrusive. His gentle touch made me know I could remain silent or I could speak.

After several minutes, my words tumbled out. But his silence and the touch of his hand had provided the healing and encouragement that enabled me to talk.

✦   ✦   ✦

As you listen, assure him that if he has trouble finding the words, you'll wait. You won't give up on him or leave the room. Assure him that no matter how terrible the things he reveals, you won't be so shocked or upset that you'll stop listening.

I'm reminded of something that happened to my late friend Katherine. We had a mutual acquaintance, and he was also her internist. She mentioned that her son had been sexually assaulted when he was ten years old. At some point her internist told her that he also had been sexually assaulted at age ten. Apparently, he described some of the horrible things that happened.

Katherine broke into tears and rushed out of his office. She was so devastated she never returned. She came to see me, and cried most of the time.

I tell this story because Katherine wasn't able to handle the truth of what she heard. That's understandable, and we can't blame her for not handling things too difficult for her.

But what about the internist?

He trusted her—perhaps he wasn't wise or, more likely, he misread her kindness and assumed it was safe for him to unload. He showed his trust by opening up to her and she rejected him.

How easy do you think it will be for him to tell another person? He's used to rejection—and probably Katherine's made it just one more. I don't want to imply that she did anything wrong. She was grieving over her own son. She liked the internist very much, but felt he had added a heavy burden on her that she couldn't handle.

So be ready for shocking stories. Do whatever it takes to listen, no matter how sad his story. If he tells you, listen. Avoid saying things like, "It's not *that* bad," resist the temptation to rage against the perpetrator. Hold back your emotions and your pain. Right now he doesn't need to have the extra burden of taking care of your feelings or worrying about your emotional state. Taking care of others and comforting them has been the burden of many abused boys. They often had to protect the feelings of older adults, and there was no one to care about them. So try to focus on him and his pain.

You might be wondering, *How can I help him?* Always keep this thought in mind: *I don't have to provide him with answers or insights.* For you merely to be available and to listen to him may not seem like much, but it's a special gift to him. For you to listen to him and love him as he is now and to let him know you accept him as he is, is the greatest healing gift you can offer. He may not be able to acknowledge it, and he may not trust it, especially at first, but don't give up on him.

He needs you. Don't let him down.

Effective Listening

Experts in communication have come up with simple rules to listen effectively. Listening is difficult, especially when the man you care for says things that shock you or gives you information you don't understand.

Before you begin, set a few basic rules for yourself. Don't answer the telephone while he's talking. Don't walk around the room, go to the restroom, serve refreshments, or begin to knit. As innocent as those things are, he can easily see them as distractions, or interpret them to mean that you're not truly interested in him or what he's saying, or that you don't want to know. They can communicate that something as minor as a telephone call is more important than his darkest secrets.

Some experts suggest you set a time frame, and that may work. It wouldn't have worked for me. I tried to choose times when I could speak to Shirley or to my friend David without interruption. If David had listened for forty-five minutes and said, "Well, time's up . . ." his remarks would have devastated me.

If you don't have time right then, offer the reason and explain that you want him to talk to you when you can be fully attentive.

Here are a few suggestions I've picked up and used in helping others. Perhaps they'll be useful for you.

Mirror His Words

This is a method attributed to Carl Rogers. You feed back to him what you hear—or think you hear. "I hear you saying . . ." It's simplistic, but it's a good way to start. You may have misunderstood and it gives him opportunity to correct you. When people talk, we don't always hear accurately, and mirroring provides a reality check for you. But it's more than feeding back the words or the message. You must listen carefully. You focus on what he says. If you can do nothing else for him, this is a powerful step.

When you mirror, you listen without interrupting and without telling him what he should have done or ought to do now. You listen carefully and nonjudgmentally. It is not correcting or advising him. If he gets names or dates wrong, let it go. Correcting him will only disrupt the flow of his thoughts and words.

Look directly at him as much as possible, and avoid looking around or staring at something else. Showing him that he has your full attention can be as simple as a nod, a pat on the hand, or some gesture that communicates that you're taking in his words. If he pauses, you can say, "Go on. Tell me more." Even to say, "Uh huh" is appropriate.

In the early days when I spoke to Shirley or David, I was so sure that they would get disgusted or tell me how stupidly I had acted as a kid. At the same time I didn't want a syrupy, maudlin voice that kept saying,

"Oh, you poor, poor child." I wanted to be able to tell my story as clearly as I remembered it, to be understood by someone I loved, and to know that despite my deeply secretive past, I was still all right in their eyes.

Validate His Story

He may not be sure you believe him—or that anyone believes him. You help him most by listening and accepting what he says. Don't challenge his memories. You're not trying to determine factual accuracy as much as you're trying to accept his memories.

Having a loved one's acceptance can be of crucial importance.

Empathize with Him

As you listen, you feel his anguish and now you respond with your feelings. It can be as simple as, "I hurt for you" or "I wish I could have been there when you went through so much pain." You think or say, "It's unfair," even if he doesn't say those words. They are your feelings and they show you understand. The problem is that many women respond to *their* feelings of pain, anger, or revulsion as they listen. They can easily lose touch with what the man feels. It happens when her feelings get so involved that she can't listen with sympathy and stay focused on him. When that happens, it's a good idea to seek professional help because a good therapist can listen objectively and still feel the pain of the other person.

As you listen, remember that men who have been sexually molested are uncomfortable talking about their experiences, especially the first few times. If he shares and you actively listen, you can provide a marvelous step in his healing.

Mull Over His Words

This is one of those times when you may need to ponder his words. This is especially significant if his revelations shocked you. Suppose he tells you his perpetrator was someone in whom *you* had absolute trust. In your shock you may say, "That blows my mind. I need time to process this part." That's being honest.

Share Your Observations—Carefully and at the Appropriate Time

If you become aware of a change in his voice or expression and think it's significant, at an appropriate time mention that fact. It's not to make a judgment but to show what you've observed. "When you spoke about your older brother, you grimaced." "When you mentioned Bill Thompson, your voice sounded angry."

By sharing your observation, you are once again saying to him, "I have listened carefully. That's why I noticed the difference."

He might be quite unaware of the change in his voice or his facial expressions. They often communicate to you feelings of which he's unaware. If you quietly point out what you observed, you aid him in his recovery.

Ineffective Listening

He needs to tell his story, and he needs for you to listen. Here are some things that can hinder the process.

False Assurances

Too often Christians say things like this:

"I know you'll get past this."

"Just keep on praying. God will answer you and set you free."

"All you need is faith. Just believe."

"God will set you free because the Bible says, 'For nothing is impossible with God.'"

"Remember that Romans 8:28 assures us that all things work together for good."

True, words from the Bible can encourage and heal—when used at the right time. Too often people quote (or even misquote) Bible verses, falling back on them as easy answers. I think it's a way they disengage *themselves* from the emotion of the moment. It's as if they can't handle honest discussion, so they throw out the first thoughts that come to them.

If you can't handle things emotionally, say so, but don't speak in clichéd phrases and Bible verses just to have something to say. Remind yourself that he was lied to in the past. Someone cunningly took advantage of him.

His abuser, too, likely manipulated him with false optimism. You want him to trust you, so avoid empty words of assurance or promises about overcoming unless you can back them up.

Negative Responses

When you refuse to accept what he says or tell him he's mistaken, you reject him. You needn't agree with everything he says, but avoid saying things like this:

"Surely you're wrong."

"You must have misunderstood what he was doing."

"Why, he wouldn't do a thing like that."

When he opens up, he'll be aware of your attitude. A negative word, facial expression, or gesture might stop him. Remember, he's carried an unspeakable burden for a long, long time, and he probably carried it alone. A negative response also includes minimizing what he says. Even if you think he's exaggerating, keep it to yourself. Just listen, because even if he's mistaken, it's what he feels. At this stage of healing, his feelings determine what's real and what isn't.

Even if you think he overreacted, say nothing. He wants to expose his feelings and his innermost thoughts. He wants to trust you. Be worthy of that trust.

Advice

Listening does not include advising. "I think you should . . ." or "You need to . . ." is needless advice and it won't help. Even if you think you know the full answer to the problem, it's better not to share it with him. Support him and encourage him to figure out the answer himself.

Even if he says, "I don't know what to do," or "What do you think I should do?" don't take the bait. He may ask the question, and you may want to give him an answer. I still urge you not to. Respond with your own question:

"What do you want to do?"

"What would be the most satisfying thing for you?"

"What's going on inside you so that you're confused about what action to take?"

This is his struggle. Rather than feed him answers, offer him compassionate listening.

Interpretation

Avoid interpreting for him, that is, telling him how he feels or how he should feel. This is his life and his pain. Let him feel and arrive at his own conclusions about himself. It's easy to insert your feelings into his story.

"That must have made you angry."

"I'll bet you were relieved to . . ."

"He didn't really love you; he was only using you for his own needs."

Don't make assumptions and don't guess.

Pushing for Details

If he's having trouble expressing or even identifying his feelings, don't probe or push him without his permission. If you're unclear about an *important* detail, ask for clarification, but overlook details that aren't significant.

Especially don't push him for details of the abuse. You may not be fully clear about what he's trying to tell you, but he knows. He may give you what I call shorthand answers because it's too painful to go into any details.

"What was he wearing?"

"What time of year was it?"

"How many minutes did the abuse last?"

"How often did the abuse take place?"

You may want to know the answers, but your questions can be disruptive or make him sense you don't believe. He doesn't need anything to stop the flow of his words. Imagine if an adult survivor is pouring out his pain to the significant woman in his life, and she wants to know the color of the wallpaper. How helpful is that?

How to Assess His Progress

At times you'll want to ask questions and know how he's doing. The first thing I suggest is that you avoid questions that he can answer with yes or no. Ask what we call open-ended questions. Begin questions with words such as *what* or *how*:

"What can I do to make it easier for you to talk?"

"What would you like me to do to help you?"

"How do you feel when you talk to me?"

"How do you feel after we've talked?"

Such simple questions aren't intrusive. They show your emotional involvement and your eagerness to help. They allow him to respond as simply as he chooses. He may want to elaborate, and the choice is his.

The more you can encourage him to be open and to talk about the sexual assault, the easier you make it for him to heal. And the more he realizes he doesn't have to be afraid to talk to you.

32

PRAY FOR HIM

Most likely he won't be able to pray about his assault in your presence because he has lived so long with his secret shame. Let him know you're praying for him. And pray aloud in his presence if you can.

Here's something helpful I've done. I've not only promised others that I'd pray for them but also asked, "Specifically, how do you want me to pray?" Sometimes he may not know the answer.

Here are two statements for you to think about and ponder as you pray. First, he didn't have a normal childhood. The abuse interrupted his development. In some areas he hasn't developed and may seem fixated in childhood. In other areas, he may have pushed ahead into adulthood. In my case, I felt an enormous responsibility to take care of others. From childhood, I was the one who reached out. As I look back, I think it was because I did what I wished someone had done for me: I wished someone had cared for me and protected me.

Second, he probably grew up feeling isolated, vulnerable, with little sense of self-worth. He probably feels at least a little that way today, even if he doesn't say so. He may need you to tell him often that he is, indeed, worthwhile.

A writer-friend named Rich fits into this category. He didn't ask for anyone to encourage him, but he'd make statements about what an excellent writer he was. Whenever he received the slightest praise from an editor, he spread the word and probably embellished it.

At first he irritated me but as I befriended him, I saw his neediness.

He felt worthless and empty, and his congratulating himself was his way of saying, "If you won't tell me I'm worthwhile, I'll tell you."

Was Rich aware of what he did? I don't think so. I also know that the closer our friendship grew, the less he needed to extol his own talents. Observe the adult survivor in your life. In what areas is he weak, afraid, or unsure? In what areas boastful, controlling, or stern? To help him, look beyond his behavior, seek the person behind it, look for the hurting child and pray for him.

In addition to praying for him each day, let him *know* that you're praying for him. For some of us who hurt, to know that others—even one person—prays for us each day can be comforting. A few years ago I had a lengthy conversation with Mike, a sales rep for a publishing house. Without my asking, he opened up and told me of being molested by his Sunday school teacher. We sat in the corner in a convention center, away from the crowds. He turned and faced the window as tears slid down his cheeks.

I reached over and laid my hand on top of his. "I can't heal you," I said, "but I can pray for God to heal you." I prayed quietly for him.

When we finished, I said, "I promise to pray for you every day for one year."

"You would do that?"

"Of course I will," I said.

Mike grabbed me and hugged me so tightly, I found it difficult to breathe.

I e-mailed him four or five times during the year to encourage him and remind him that I continued to pray for him daily. Mike didn't answer any of the e-mails, but that was all right: I had promised to pray for him, and that's what I did.

A year later at the same convention, Mike saw me as I stood in line at a restaurant. He left his table and rushed to me. He embraced me warmly. When he released me, he said, "This has been a terrible year for me, but one thing kept me going. Many times I wanted to give up, and I would remind myself, 'Cec is praying for me today.' That gave me the courage to keep on."

The point of my story is to encourage you to pray for the man in your life who was sexually assaulted in childhood. Pray for him fervently and daily. Even if you say nothing else to him, let him know, "I'm praying for you every day." You might get more specific such as, "I pray daily for your full recovery."

That may not seem like a big thing to many; however, it's a big thing to those of us who struggled through childhood. We felt alone and we believed that no one cared about us.

When we know there are those who care—even if it's only one person—it makes a tremendous difference. It makes us able to say, "I'm not alone."

— 33 —

RESPECT HIS PRIVACY

If the adult survivor in your life tells you his story, don't tell anyone— *not anyone*—without his permission. For most of us who were molested, trust is an important issue, maybe the most important. In childhood, someone he trusted betrayed him; as an adult, he doesn't want to be betrayed again by someone he trusts.

Remind yourself that he has the right to speak, and he also has the right to remain silent. If he opens up and tells you his story, it says he trusts you. If you feel you must tell someone, ask his permission. If it's too big for you to hold alone, tell him what you want to do.

If you share his story with even your most trusted friend, unless he gives you permission to do so, you will have violated his privacy. Even if your friend promises she won't tell another soul, what if she does? What if she confides only in her closest confidant, her husband? Someone tells someone else and eventually it gets back to him. However well-intentioned you may have been, he'll be victimized all over again.

In the early days of my recovery, when I talked to my wife and my friend David about my abuse, I would have been deeply wounded had I learned they told anyone. Eventually I was able to speak out and talk freely about my abuse. And later I didn't mind if they told others. But not at first—not in the first months of my healing. And some men may never want others to know, so please seriously look at the issue of his privacy.

He has the right to his own secrets. He has the right to privacy.

✦ ✦ ✦

In respecting his privacy, there are two important things for you to remember. First, be loyal. Assault victims struggle over trusting people. Most perpetrators were people they trusted—neighbors, older boys, or church leaders. He knows betrayal too well. If you tell anyone *without his permission*, even a small part of his secret, even to someone you're sure you can trust, then whom can *he* trust? He'll be alone again.

Second, help him trust. In this book I've touched on the topic of trust several times and it's probably the most significant issue for adult survivors. As children we naturally assumed that those who provided for us would take care of us. That circle of trust included extended family members, neighbors, and professionals. Then something happened to make us lose our naiveté. We were molested. Whether it was a parent, a neighbor, or a person in authority, someone failed and hurt each of us. After that, we became suspicious, sometimes cynical. We probably didn't know how to trust kind words or caring gestures and often looked for the selfish motives behind them.

Everyone won't betray his secrets, but how does he know that? If you allow him his privacy without intruding, without demanding things he doesn't want to talk about, you help him trust. You can help him learn to trust others because you showed your trustworthiness. You showed him that it's safe and, because of you, he may be able to take the next step forward.

— 34 —

LET HIM MOURN

Not only was he assaulted, but it was done by someone he trusted. That trusted individual stole his childhood innocence. Every child deserves to be loved and nurtured. He never had that opportunity. He can never have it, but he can experience self-acceptance if you allow him to feel sadness and grief.

Sometimes outsiders don't understand the grieving process. Think of it this way. We survived childhood. We learned techniques and forms of behavior that worked to get us to adulthood. They may not be appropriate for us today, but they're part of our learned behavior.

I used two techniques to survive. My father was a brutal man when he was drunk, which was every weekend. One week he'd rage over something that at another time wouldn't bother him. I never knew when he would erupt. So as soon as he and I encountered each other, whether it was after he got out of work, before breakfast, or outside in the yard, I had to size up the situation quickly. Or, as I would say it today, "I had to intuit his mood." If I was correct and he was nearing an explosion, I used the technique of staying as far away from him as possible. Or I kept my mouth shut and said nothing to upset him. I became proficient at intuiting his mood.

The second technique I used, and so did my baby brother, Chuck, was that we didn't feel the pain when he beat us. I can only say that we were able to mentally leave our bodies so that he didn't hurt us. We screamed to convince him that he hurt us, but we didn't feel it.

After I grew up, it took a long time for me to feel physical pain of any kind. I never thought about it until I went to a chiropractor the first time. He kept doing something on my back and asking, "Does that hurt?"

Each time I truthfully said, "No."

When he finished the exam, he said, "You have a remarkably high tolerance for pain."

That surprised me because it wasn't something of which I'd been aware. I called Chuck on the phone a couple of days later about a different matter. Before I hung up, I related the chiropractor's words.

Chuck laughed. "Of course," he said. "Don't you remember? We decided not to let the beatings hurt."

I'd forgotten.

In adulthood, pain can be a warning of something seriously wrong with our bodies. So what enabled some of us to survive then, can impede our lives now. But we've grown up with our protective devices. We hugged them tightly and they enabled us to survive. An attitude of "You can't hurt me; I won't let you hurt me" is an example of how we can eventually become invulnerable. If we shut down our pains and grief, we shut off the positive sides of our personality as well.

Grieving can be a significant step forward for him, and the grief might be because he feels he must give up something—something on which he depended. That something was like his childhood security blanket. He might be helped if he gave it up eventually, but he resists giving it up and needs to grieve in order to let it go. Grieving, then, is an element in his healing. Grieving means that he can finally say goodbye to the unhealthy parts of himself.

Recognize that all people grieve in their own way and at their own pace. It's understandable that loved ones want to nudge the survivor and yearn for him to get over his past. But he may not be able to move as rapidly as they'd like. Merely to have knowledge of the past or of the pain doesn't cure him of either. The knowledge provides awareness so that healing can take place.

Instead of wishing you could help him get over his grief, you may need to remind yourself, "He's doing the best he can. He might be feeling overwhelmed by losses. Right now he needs my patience and my support."

It's important for him to concentrate on the past. He's trying to make sense of his world and bring healing to his childhood. It won't happen quickly. He may never be fully healed. I hope that's not true for the man in your life, but there might be issues over which he'll struggle all his life. They probably won't cause him the sharp pains of the past, but they'll be present, showing up in his behavior.

As a survivor of sexual molestation, he needs to confront the cause of his pain in his own way. He may need to mourn over his powerlessness. Even though he did the best he could as a child, he was traumatized. Let him feel his pain. Let him mourn over the reality that he didn't deserve the treatment, over the loss of his childhood, over the loss of the familiar ways he copes with pain.

If you remain steadfast, there's hope that the grieving will enable him to realize that he doesn't deserve the guilt, the shame, and the self-loathing he's felt through the years. Those feelings belong to the abuser but he—as the victim, as the innocent child—took them on because of the silence and the betrayal. So let him mourn for that child too.

— 35 —

BE HONEST WITH HIM

He was victimized by false words. His assailant probably called him "special" and said, "I love you," and later abandoned him. Because of the gross deception of his past, he's probably quick to pick up on dishonesty.

If you're honest, he'll learn to believe you care and that he matters to you. If you're sad when he talks about what happened and want to cry, do it, but take care about what you say. He's known false emotion and deceitful words. He might never challenge you, but he might be suspicious when you speak. Because he probably heard words such as, "I love you," and "I'll always take care of you," he'll detect any of your words that are false.

"You're special," were words he may have heard when he was young. Those were words Mr. Lee spoke to me. Only after I got in touch with my abuse was I ready to grasp that he lied to me. I wasn't special; I was just a hurt child. And Mr. Lee caused the hurt.

Be honest, but don't focus on how *you feel*. Some of us molested kids learned to be caregivers of those who manipulated us. If the man in your life is like that, in the past he might have responded to expressions of sadness or loneliness. He may have reached out to those who said, "I need you." Those who manipulated him might have said something like, "You're the only person to whom I can turn."

Try to listen to his emotions, facial expressions, and gestures and not only his words. Because you know him, you can sense how deeply he feels. Listen uncritically as he talks about the abuse or the abuser. Does he blame himself? Does he make excuses for the perpetrator?

Don't try to correct him and tell him how he *should* feel, but in a gentle-but-firm voice you can help him by being honest. Here are things you can say:

"It was not your fault."

"You did nothing wrong. You were a child of seven and he was a man of forty-two. You couldn't run away or fight."

"You were set up because he was determined to abuse you."

"You were a defenseless child and powerless to stop him."

If the adult survivor talks about the perpetrator's expressing love for him, don't contradict or argue. Instead, ask a few questions. As much as possible, keep your voice neutral.

"How did he show you love? Did he show it by keeping the loving act hidden? By pleading with you not to tell anyone? By saying, 'This is our secret'?"

Such statements show the man in your life that you feel compassion and sympathy for him.

In the early days of my recovery, my wife made it clear that she would stand by me and support me. A few times Shirley cried when I told her of recovered memories. Sometimes she hugged me and held me. That's all I needed. That's all most abused men need.

He deserves honest responses. If you want to be part of his healing, your honesty is one of the most powerful things you can give to him.

36

PAY ATTENTION TO HIS EMOTIONS

The adult survivor's feelings are more important than the events themselves. Perhaps that sounds obvious, but I've encountered people who want to pry and soak up all the information. "Tell me everything," they said. It was intrusive. I sensed they wanted to hear lurid details more than they wanted to help me.

You don't want to show indifference to his past. You help him most by simple responses. When he tells you a particularly graphic experience, don't press for details (unless you need clarification). Instead, focus on him.

Try to sense what's going on inside him as he talks. "How did you feel when that happened?" A direct question like that keeps the camera pointing at him. Let him tell you as much or as little as he chooses.

Look at his face when he talks. Sometimes the facial expressions and the words don't match. Here's an example. As I've already mentioned, for four years I belonged to a group of six men that met every Thursday—without missing. All of us had been wounded by some form of abuse.

One evening, I shared a particularly painful experience about the old man who rented a room from us. He had molested my older sister and me. When I finished, John said, "You told us a sad story, but you're smiling."

His words shocked me. I had no awareness of the smile. He helped me face the fact that I told a true and powerful account, but I still held back. I assume I smiled unconsciously as part of my way to prepare for the other five men to reject me.

Help Him See His Emotions

As I wrote in part 1 of this book, adult survivors of childhood sexual abuse often are not in touch with our own emotions. To survive childhood, many of us learned to deny or minimize our pain. Before the man in your life can heal, however, he needs to experience his own emotions.

By paying attention to his emotions, you can help *him* pay attention to his emotions. Commend him for learning to survive by ignoring his pain. Help him recognize his emotions. You can help him process his feelings.

A suggestion that some have found helpful in doing that is to say something to him like this:

+ "Remember when you interviewed for a job and hoped the company would offer the position to you? You felt *sad* when you learned they chose someone else."
+ "Remember when your mother forgot your birthday? That was a *sad* time for you."
+ "Did I *hurt your feelings* when I . . . ? Are you feeling all right about what I said to you?"

Let him answer. He may try to avoid an answer, and you needn't argue, but you've opened the door for him.

Put yourself in his place: how would you feel if someone claimed that you felt an emotion that you didn't really feel? Defensive? Or how did you react when someone pointed out an emotion of which you weren't aware? Suppose someone said to you, "You were really upset over his words; your face was contorted with anger," but you were unaware of that physical expression. Would you feel that person had invaded your privacy? Quite likely, especially if it was someone you either didn't know well or hadn't learned to trust.

Try to make it easier for him to open up. You might say something like, "I may have misread the expression on your face, but you seemed shocked and hurt. I'm not pushing you to say anything, but I want you to know that's what I saw. If I read it correctly, I want you to know I'm sorry you're hurt."

One woman said she did just that. When she would observe her husband's body language and realize he wasn't aware of his feelings, she would say softly, "The way you stand makes me think you're upset. If you want to think about it or talk about it, it's all right."

Demonstrate Your Own Emotions

Another approach to help the man in your life recognize his own feelings is to demonstrate *your* feelings. Be open about your disappointments, anger, and pain. As *you* become more open and vulnerable to him, you give *him* permission to open up as well. You might say, "You know when she treated you rudely, it hurt me. I saw the pain on your face. How did you feel about what went on?"

I'll share an experience here. David Morgan is a man I like very much and we became good friends. He was easy to talk to but he rarely said anything about how *he* felt. At first I thought he was a passive individual.

One time we talked and I said something—I don't remember what I said—and I saw a flicker of pain in David's eyes. I had never observed anything like that before. I told him, and his eyes moistened but he didn't cry. Later, he told me that it had been a powerful moment for him. "That's when I understood your irrefutable love."

That's what you can do for the adult survivor in your life. If you can sense what he may not be able to consciously reveal, and tell him, you prove your compassion and love.

Recognize "Magical Thinking"

Some of us survivors have believed in what I call magical thinking: *If she really loved me, she'd know how I felt.* If you suspect that the man you care for thinks this way, talk to him about it: "I can't read your mind.

I can only know what you tell me." You may need to help him learn to speak his feelings.

If you recognize his behavior patterns—such as shallow breathing, sweating, or pacing—you might ask, "Do you realize you're fidgeting? Are you feeling anxious or nervous about something?" Encourage him to talk about his feelings. It may take time for him to learn to do that, but it's worth the effort.

Be Patient; Change Is Possible

As he opens up, help him to be patient with himself. If you encourage him and express your loving support, you make it easier for him to move ahead in his healing.

In adulthood, he can leave the old ways behind of separating himself from his feelings. If he internally grasps the truth of 2 Corinthians 5:17, that the old has been wiped away and he has become new, he has the promise. He may need you to help him enter into the new way of recognizing and expressing his feelings. The safer the path and the more loving the method, the easier it is for him to make those changes.

Encourage him to believe he's not to blame that he's lost touch with his feelings. Rather his behavior was learned as a brave, struggling child who figured out a way to make it through the morass and pain. He deserves admiration and love. He negotiated a way out of insanity and did it even when he wasn't aware of what he did.

He survived that childhood, and he needs to know that change is possible. He needs a loving environment that promotes change. If he trusts that his behavior doesn't make you love him less, he can change and grow. You can enable him to take those healing steps.

He wants to be more than a survivor; he wants to be victorious. He needs your help.

37

DON'T LET HIM SELF-PUNISH

At some point, the adult survivor in your life may denigrate or belittle himself.

"Why did it take so long for me to get help?"

"I failed again, didn't I? That's the way I am."

"I'm not worth your taking time to listen."

"I'll mess up again. I always do."

It's not enough, then, that he feel your compassion for him; he needs to feel compassion toward himself. And you may need to help him do that. Because he was abused and treated badly as a child, he may have fallen into the pattern of making degrading comments about himself. As long as he says such things, he continues to punish himself for something that was done to him. Help him move beyond that stage in his recovery.

My friend David helped me on this one. I sometimes said harsh things about myself. Several times he stopped me and with kindness reminded me what I was doing. One time he said, "Think of the little boy inside yourself—the kid who was molested and treated badly. Can't you show him a little compassion?"

After David left, I sat down in an easy chair, relaxed, and closed my eyes. I tried to see myself as a kid at the time Mr. Lee molested me. I talked to that little boy and told him I was sorry. I said he had been hurt during his childhood, and I didn't want to add to that pain. I asked him to forgive me.

I repeated that kind of dialogue with myself on three different occasions before I fully embraced that hurt boy of my childhood. Because I could feel compassion for him and show it to him, it brought healing to me, the adult. I stopped saying belittling things about myself. Once in a while a self-put-down slips out, but I've made significant progress in recent years.

"Why—"

The man you care for may still struggle with those issues of self-esteem. When he makes self-deprecating statements such as, "Why did I wait so long? Why didn't I get help sooner?" don't even attempt to answer the question. You may have even wondered yourself why he waited so long. Here are a few of the many possible reasons:

Distortion. He may not have thought of the childhood event as molestation. Maybe he couldn't face the truth of what had happened to him. Maybe he thought it occurred in every family. It takes time to correct the lies that were told to him, lies that made sexual abuse seem like something quite different.

Fear. Maybe the man in your life was afraid. Although the abusive behavior is over and far behind him, it can still feel dangerous. He might still tighten up when he relives those events.

Helplessness. He might not have known he could do anything about his molestation. He may have assumed it was something with which he had to live.

Hopelessness. Maybe it didn't occur to him that he could be healed. Women have been speaking out about rape and abuse for at least two decades. Other than abuse by priests in the Catholic church, most people haven't heard much about boys being abused or about programs set up to help them. If he didn't think it would do any good, why would he try to get help?

Poor self-image. Perhaps he felt like an evil person who didn't deserve help.

But the *why* isn't important. Remind him that there are solid reasons for his not dealing with the issue of abuse. All adult survivors start the recovery process in different ways and at different points in our lives. Tell him, "This is your recovery time now."

The point is, hashing over the many possible reasons is not productive and just stalls his telling his story. A simple response, "You're seeking help now," is probably all you need to say. Another simple response might be something like, "You were hurt and you had no one who really cared before. You did the best you could." Regardless of how he second-guesses himself, help him not to condemn or blame himself. "It's good that you're seeking help now rather than waiting even longer." In short, the time wasn't right or he wasn't ready. For him to condemn himself for that fact doesn't help him.

"But—"

No matter what words he follows with, assure him that God loves him and you love him. Tell him you refuse to listen to his self-deprecating words. Tell him, "It hurts me when you say terrible things about yourself. It hurts me because they're not true."

At a men's conference in Seattle in the early 1990s, a seventy-two-year-old man spoke briefly at the plenary session. He said he had come to terms with his abusive childhood only that year. "I've lost a lot of time getting here," he said, "but now that I'm here, I'm running fast."

The applause must have lasted a full two minutes.

The man you care for needs to know that healing is possible for him too. But no one can accomplish it alone. He needs help. As an adult survivor, he needs to test his perceptions against his own experiences and those of others. A self-help group would be an ideal place to do that, but he may resist the idea of participating in a group. He may feel he's not ready to trust other men in the group, that his story is more sordid than theirs, that they may use what he tells them as ammunition to hurt him.

He's mistaken, of course, but for you to tell him that is not productive. Rather, if you want to help the man you care for, show him that *you* are worthy of his trust. You might say, "I can understand why you're not ready to trust. As a child you instinctively trusted others, but someone betrayed you and you've probably lost the ability to trust."

Then by the things you say and do, you show your love and compassion, and you help him to trust you. You can't change what happened to him in the past, but you can love him unconditionally in the present. Loving unconditionally means accepting the stage he's in now. Imagine how other men in a self-help group would respond to the man you care for if he were to tell his story. Would they be shocked? Would they laugh? Would they tell him he was mistaken or try to minimize what happened? Would they agree that he should have done more to protect himself? Absolutely not.

If you respond to him the way you think other adult survivors might respond, eventually he will be able to trust others. He needs you to stand by him to help him. For him to build a solid foundation, your understanding and your trust in him must be part of that foundation. If you support him emotionally and with compassion, he can build self-esteem, positive relationships, and embrace a richer, fuller, more spiritual life.

Healing isn't easy to accomplish, but it can be an exciting journey. Despite my tears and pain, I found it so. I say "despite my tears and pain," because that's how I would have said it in those early days of healing. Today I would say it differently. I learned to feel. I learned to connect my body with my mind and my emotions.

I also learned that I wasn't alone. Until Shirley and David armed me for my struggle, I felt alone. I had a deep, sad part of myself that I couldn't share with anyone. Shortly after my healing began, I had a dream. I saw a concrete vault that was under water. I swam to it and around it several times. There seemed to be no lock, but it wouldn't open. I pounded on one wall and nothing happened. Then I pounded the concrete with both fists. A door that had been previously hidden opened slowly, and I swam into the vault.

That was the dream, and I knew it was a message for me. The vault represented the hidden, submerged pains and memories of childhood. Until I struck with both fists, there was no way in. Once I pounded the wall, it opened for me.

That dream encouraged me to realize that I was going to get inside that vault. I would win. I didn't know what I would be like or even who I would be when I came back out, but I believed that life would never be as bleak and lonely as it had been.

I was right.

The man in your life has enough battles. Don't let his self-punishment be one of them.

38

ALLOW HIS INCONSISTENCIES

The adult survivor was robbed of the innocence of childhood and he's trying to find himself. He may not know who he really is, and that not knowing is the beginning of self-discovery.

Here's an example to explain what I mean. About a year into my recovery, I'd reached the place where I didn't mind Shirley talking about my background, and I told her it was all right to mention it around others. One evening, we ate dinner with another couple whom we'd known for several years. During the evening, Shirley said to them, "I don't know who Cec is anymore. He used to be predictable."

I beamed when I heard those words. She said the perfect thing: I *had* changed. I thought I'd changed, but I wasn't aware if she'd noticed it. She had, but she just hadn't dwelt on my being inconsistent with the Cec to whom she'd been married for years. She didn't understand who I was, but she did grasp that I had changed. Rather than make an issue about the changes, she had accepted them.

You need to be aware of this fact about the man in your life who was once abused: if he grows, he will change. For a period of time, Shirley had to adjust to a different me. I've been grateful to God that she was willing to move out of her sense of who I was and to allow for change or for new inconsistencies.

If the man you care for changes, it's because he's dealing with his issues. They're not your problems, your fault, or your issues. He might temporarily withdraw from you or shut you out—and it's not because of something you've done. Accept that it's his way of coping with his situation and integrating healing into his life.

Especially allow him to numb out. I discussed in chapter 17 that numbness is common for those of us who were abused. When during our adult lives we are in situations that cause powerful emotions, we become like observers who watch the action take place. We become emotionally divorced from the situation—which was a significant coping skill during our childhoods. Experts call that dissociating from a traumatic event.

For some of us, an experience so overwhelms us that our minds can't hold together the traumatic parts. Someone said it was like putting all the pain in a glass jar and storing it away—even while the painful experience is taking place. It means we disconnect from our immediate experience. We lose all sense of emotions and physical reactions. At a time when you might expect the man you care for to show a lot of emotion, he—in a way inconsistent with the moment—may show none. He might have used that method to live through a painful childhood.

Another type of inconsistency is that one day he might seem to have moved forward and the next day to have slipped back. He might feel one way on a particular day and differently on another. Let him be inconsistent. That happens. The pain might be so intense he needs to retreat to a safer place, or safer position. Avoid pointing out to him, "Yesterday you said . . . but today . . ." He has to struggle in his own way and might need to retreat occasionally.

Until he can open that sealed jar and get back in touch with the pain, he might be involved in what seems like self-defeating activities. This is where I've seen strong inconsistencies in men. Sometimes they receive compliments and don't know how to process them.

"Was he insulting me?"

"What did he mean by that?"

"Why doesn't she like me? What did I do to her?"

As he opens the stored-away jar and re-experiences his emotions, he can become more consistent.

He might also ask questions about being understood, even about mundane matters. It might seem inconsistent to you that he'd be unsure of something he was sure about only a few days ago. How should you respond if he asks, "Does that make sense?" If it does, say so. If it's unclear, tell him. Remember, honesty is the rule to follow. You may have to ask him to clarify or to say it again.

If you're able, you might also ask him *the question behind the question.* That is, we sometimes show inconsistency by asking a question, but it's not the *real* question. In chapter 12 I write about Ken, a budding writer who asked, "Is there any money in this business?" What he really wanted to ask is, "Can I make a living at writing?"

I couldn't answer that, of course, because there were too many variables. How good a writer is Ken? How motivated is he? How aggressive is he in promoting and marketing himself? How willing is he to learn? Those are questions Ken has to ask and to answer himself.

Help the man you care for figure out the questions he really wants to ask, and by doing so you help him answer questions he can't yet ask. If that sounds abstract, let me put it in a nutshell: Ask yourself, *How can he be confident that his perceptions are correct?* Remember, his abuser distorted reality.

✦　✦　✦

Even if he appears to be strong, that might be only a facade. Inside, his world might be falling apart. Does he need at times to dominate? It may not be in words. It might be in actions or even through showing a lack of interest. Or at other times he might be the one that's easily influenced or led astray. If either or both fit him, don't let his behavior discourage you, and don't take it personally. He needs someone to turn to when he seems inconsistent even to himself. He needs someone like you.

Try to understand that he's struggling to separate the past from the present. He can't move far into the future until he's made sense of and received healing from the past. Accept that he's doing the best he knows how for his own recovery. He might need time alone. His moods will probably fluctuate. The more you encourage him to take the time he needs, and the more you tell him how glad you are that he's working so hard at healing, the more progress he'll make.

39

BE CAREFUL ABOUT TOUCH

I was one of about three hundred who attended a men's convention a few years ago in Pittsburgh. Three of us came in late and couldn't sit together. I found an empty seat by myself. Midway through the evening, the speaker asked us to spend a few minutes greeting those around us. A lot of laughing and hugging went on.

The man on my left smiled and hugged me. Something about his touch wasn't right. I couldn't have explained it objectively to anyone, but something about the embrace startled me, and I felt uncomfortable.

At the end of the evening, the same man walked behind me as we exited the building. He engaged me in small talk. I remember only that he said his name was Kenneth (and his name tag said that anyway) and he lived in Kansas City. I saw my two friends and said, "My friends are waiting. See you later," or something like that.

Just then, Kenneth grabbed me and embraced me—in itself that didn't bother me. But I had the same odd feeling when he touched me. This time his fingers went into my belt loops and pulled me tight. That felt even stranger. When he released me, I pulled away and hurried to my friends. I avoided Kenneth for the next two days.

Good Touch and Bad Touch

From that experience, I formulated a theory. There is good touch and there is bad touch. As children, male survivors were touched in inappropriate ways. Some of us became hypersensitive to physical embraces and knew the difference immediately. As adults, we probably have no problem discerning the difference, but unexpected touch, whether good or bad, may still trigger negative reactions.

Here's a good rule: Don't touch him unless you're assured that it's appropriate for him and appropriate at that time. I write this because, for many years, I jumped when anyone gave me an unexpected hug. People have come up behind me and playfully surprised me with a bear hug. I wasn't able to take it playfully.

One time I stood on a street corner, reading the playbill for a movie. Someone grabbed my waist from behind. In a reflex action, I twirled around and my fist flew. I bloodied his nose. "You startled me," I yelled in my defense. (I also apologized for hurting him.)

Many of us survivors have a quick reflex when it comes to touch. We're easily startled and jump or scream when we experience an unexpected touch.

Even among couples, you need to decide what is appropriate. His comfort level may change from moment to moment, so talk to him about your touching him. Ask him how he feels when you touch him without his being aware of your intention.

Women used to tell me that when certain men hugged them, they felt he was coming on to them. As a survivor of sexual abuse, I now understand.

Violation and Control

Some men are afraid of physical touch because of experiences associated with their molestation. The man in your life may be one of them. The primary violation was related to his body, and he might need to learn that it is *his body* and he has control over it. Let him decide when, how, and from whom he will accept touch.

Talk to him about touch. "Because you were touched in unwelcome ways when you were a child, how do you feel about being touched now?" Ask him to help you know when and how to touch him. I hope you can see how empowering that can be for him. He was a victim before, but now he is in control of being touched. Your willingness to let him guide you in the way you touch him makes it easier for you, but it's also healing for him.

The men's group that I belonged to in Louisville met on Saturday mornings at a wing of a local hospital. The wing was closed on weekends, and we had a large room with no one to disturb us. A few of us decided to stand in front of the building where we met and greet other men, especially to welcome newcomers. Men came to the gathering for many reasons and from various backgrounds, and we wanted to be open and friendly and to help them feel welcome.

I was careful not to hug a man until I knew it was all right with him. One of our greeters, Don, had been so uplifted by "male skin touching," as he put it, he indiscriminately hugged every man who came. A few of the men flinched. I once tried to explain to Don that not everyone welcomed the hug.

"Maybe not, but they need it," he said.

"But they may not realize they need it."

He shrugged and continued to embrace every man who came toward the door.

Even though I don't know the reason some flinched, I understand what an invasion it might have felt like. If they had been sexually abused in childhood, an embrace meant violation of their bodies. Even though those men were adults, that didn't mean they were totally free from their past. It meant they were probably embraced only when it involved sex.

That was certainly true in my life. The only male touch I knew was that of Mr. Lee. My parents never demonstrated tenderness toward each other in our presence. Not once do I remember my father hugging me or showing warmth. What did I understand about physical touch?

The first time I was hugged in a nonsexual way I was twenty-three years old. I visited a church for the first time, and I had hardly gotten inside when a large, one-armed man greeted me at the door. Before I could say anything, he embraced me. Later I realized that Bernard was developmentally disabled and wanted to hug everybody. But that first time his actions scared me.

In time, of course, I learned to accept hugs and to give them. But some men don't reach that stage. For them, a male's physical touch is too painful a reminder. Their bodies were mistreated. They were objectified.

Flashbacks

For some adult survivors, what he perceives as an inappropriate touch might even trigger a flashback. In chapter 7 I write more in depth about flashbacks. Here, though, are a few suggestions when the man you care for has flashbacks, whether triggered by touch or any other stimuli:

Remind him that what he feels isn't real—it may have been a traumatic experience in the past, but it is not true now. He survived the first time; he can survive it again because he's more mature and stronger. This flashback won't stay; it will go away. Flashbacks intrude only briefly, but remind him that they are unresolved traumatic experiences that carry a heavy burden of emotion.

Listen quietly and attentively when he speaks or describes a flashback. Say something to him like this: "There's nothing wrong with you. Remind yourself of that if you have doubts. You aren't crazy and this is a normal emotional response." You may need to say to him softly, "You're safe. Nothing can hurt you now."

Many of us survivors are easily startled and act reflexively at an unexpected touch. Try not to take it personally if at times you feel like he's rejecting you. He's not rejecting you; he's reacting to a painful past.

— 40 —

DON'T PUSH HIM TO FORGIVE

"My Sunday school teacher told me I had to forgive," Tom said. "He said that if I didn't, God would hold my sin against me. And he quoted: 'If I regard [hold] iniquity in my heart, the Lord will not hear me'" (Ps. 66:18 KJV). At the insistence of the teacher and a church deacon, Tom went to the front of the church, fell on his knees, and confessed that he had not been forgiving. A number of people knelt around him and prayed for him.

When Tom finished his story he looked directly at me. "Maybe I went through the right steps, but I didn't feel as if I'd forgiven my abuser." He paused and said, "In fact, I didn't want to forgive him—at least not then."

I know that script. Too many well-intentioned people want us to rush into forgiveness before we're ready. Yes, forgiving is a *part* of healing, but a lot of people make forgiveness and reconciliation the *goal* of healing. *Don't urge him toward premature forgiving.* To him, when someone makes him feel that he must forgive or he's not a good Christian, that's one more form of manipulation. When he's ready, he will forgive.

Just as you accept the pace at which he releases his pain, accept the pace at which he's ready to forgive his perpetrator. I believe in both, but to push, urge, or insist on it can become dangerous to his healing. When he's healed enough, he'll want to forgive. He's carried the pain a long time and it doesn't dissolve immediately. For some men, it's years before they can release the pain, and years before they can forgive.

What "Forgive" *Doesn't* Mean

Many nonbelievers, as well as believers, don't fully grasp biblical forgiveness. To forgive doesn't mean that the victim needs to seek a relationship with the perpetrator. The offender needs the grace of God, but that doesn't mean the victim has to be the dispenser. The victim forgives because God's grace is at work in him.

To forgive doesn't mean that the offender's behavior was acceptable. It wasn't and it will never be acceptable. Forgiveness doesn't mean that the victim concedes that the perpetrator didn't mean to hurt him. Of course the victim was hurt.

To forgive doesn't mean that the crime—and it is a crime—has been wiped away or that the guilty won't ever be held accountable. To forgive doesn't condone or overlook the abuser's action.

Why Forgive?

"Why should I forgive him?" During the year I spent in the state-sponsored group for survivors, I heard that question several times. At first, several of us tried to answer the question.

One day, one of the group said, "That's a good question. When you know the answer yourself, you're ready to forgive."

I agreed with him.

As I've pondered the issue of forgiving perpetrators, here are reasons I've come up with to forgive:

+ I now have freedom from the painful controls of my past. They no longer torment me.
+ I have decreased the likelihood that my anger will be misdirected toward others who aren't responsible for the abuse, including myself.
+ I have reduced the fear that I might have violent impulses.
+ I grow in the process. I grow in relationship with other people. As

long as I withhold forgiveness, I'm isolated from many things in my own emotional life. The stronger the anger and pain, the less open I am to positive emotions.

When Forgiveness Will Occur

Some men don't resolve the forgiveness issue. Until they perceive God's grace and forgiveness toward them, they can't truly forgive. Until they recognize they are made whole *only* by divine help, they can't push away the anger and grudges they hold.

He's ready to forgive when he no longer blames himself for the abuse or punishes himself for what he did or didn't do. Getting to that point is a gradual process and doesn't occur at one moment. As he learns to accept himself as he is and begins to treat himself with respect and affection, he may come to realize that forgiveness is an act of compassion toward himself.

It took time for me to grasp that. Whenever the topic of molestation came up, I thought of Mr. Lee and what his actions had done to me. At one point I said, "He ruined my life." He didn't ruin my life but he made it extremely painful for me. After I finally tired of exerting energy toward hating him, I chose a different path to follow.

Many of us want revenge in some way, especially if the perpetrator is alive. But even if we find a way to see the other punished, our pain won't be gone. We might be satisfied that justice has reigned, but it changes nothing for us.

So keep this clearly in mind: abuse is always wrong; abuse is always sinful; abuse always hurts.

Forgiveness allows our hurts to go into the Past file. Pain doesn't have to live in the Present file or Future file. We transfer the emotional energy we used for resentment and spend it on healthy relationships.

When the man you care for is ready—when he wants to move beyond his pain—he'll forgive without being told he must. When he's ready, forgiveness becomes the obvious step.

A Refusal to Forgive

Some men have been so badly hurt, though, and have stayed so focused on their own pain, they can see nothing else but the need for justice. I've met a few men who have refused to forgive. I remember only one active church member who refused to forgive.

"I want to see him punished," he said to me several times. "I want to see his soul in hell."

I tried to argue with him from reason (my mistake), and he always had answers:

"He doesn't deserve forgiveness."

"Neither do you," I said.

"He is a man totally sold out to the Devil."

"Then let God punish him."

"He ruined my life."

"But can't Jesus help you reclaim it?"

I don't want to judge the man, and he obviously hurt. I soon realized that giving him logical responses wouldn't work. I finally raised my hand to stop him and said, "I know you hurt. I'm sorry." He started to interrupt me but I added, "I'd like to pray for you. I'd like to pray for you now and I'd like to make a prayer covenant with you." I promised that I would pray for him every day for a year.

He stopped protesting and tears slid down his cheeks.

A few months later he moved to Macon from the Atlanta area. I kept my commitment to him and e-mailed him regularly. He always acknowledged with simple words of thanks. After the year was over, he stopped responding, so I don't know what happened to him. I hope he was able to put the past where it belongs—in the past.

You may need to remind him that grief and forgiveness are processes; they are not events. He can be in one stage of dealing with his abuse over one issue and at a different stage in relation to another. He might be sad or grieving about what the abuse cost him as a child, while he takes the first steps toward forgiving the person who sinned against him.

Try to help him to remember that, in some ways, forgiveness is a self-ish act. That is, he needs to forgive for himself, not for the abuser. He needs to forgive for his own inner peace.

— *41* —

LET HIM MOVE AT HIS OWN PACE

One of my well-meaning friends bought a book about healing from sexual assault. It's one of those self-published, sixty-plus-page, fifteen-steps-to-healing books for those with "bruised emotions." Those two words are all I remember about the title. The author lays out everything in simple, logical patterns. If readers do what step one says, they will be ready for the next step. And if they go through the steps sequentially, their bruised emotions will be healed forever.

I didn't mind that the author wrote the book—that was his choice. I did mind his trying to tell me how and when to heal—that was my choice.

When I left my friend's house, I was angry. I was angry at myself for not having walked out earlier. My friend was sure the book would bring healing to me and kept insisting that if I would just go through the fifteen steps, I'd be healed.

In my most charitable moments, I admit there is some good advice in the book. Some. It's what I call a book of formulas. And none of us operate our emotions by formula. We're human beings with variations. No two men heal the same way or over the same period of time.

The best thing you can do for the man you love is to let him heal at *his* pace. Healing is made up of many elements, or steps, but rather than project the steps for him to take, let him decide which steps to take and when to take them. Step 6 or 7 in the book read something like this: "Now is the time for him to express his anger at the person who abused him." A couple of steps later it was time to forgive.

Really? How did the author know it was time? Or how did he know the victim wanted to forgive? For some of us, forgiveness takes years.

I encourage you to help the man in your life through all the steps of healing, but he must set the pace. If he doesn't walk as fast as you'd like, remind yourself that this is *his* journey, *his* life. He endured great trauma and it will take time—probably years—for a full and total recovery. Lectures won't speed the process, but your assurances that you're emotionally available can. You can encourage him to take the first meaningful steps toward healing and, you can stay at his side. Don't expect a quick fix. He's probably tried that himself. When he senses that you won't turn against him if he's slow in healing, he might be ready to take another step.

Let him see by your words and attitudes that you accept his reluctance, for instance, to let go of the coping mechanisms that enabled him to survive. They were created by the wounded child, and he did the best he could. You don't want him to fool himself into thinking, for another example, that facing the past erases it. Because you love the abused man in your life, you don't want to force him to face that past before he's ready. But you can hold his hand when he chooses to open the door himself.

If he understands your love for him, he'll turn to you more easily when he needs encouragement along the way. And your affection must be genuine; he can probably sense if you're taking a real interest in his struggle or if you're just going through the motions. You don't need to be an expert; you don't need to know a great deal about abuse. You do need to love him and manifest your love in such a way that he knows he can open up to you.

As he opens to you, you can help him to stay focused on *his* recovery. You can remind him that he doesn't need to spare your feelings or to protect you. You can remind him that his painful emotions are part of the healing. And there's one more thing you might need to tell him: they *will* decrease.

Avoid phrases, though, that begin with, "You need to . . ." Rather than stand behind him, pushing in a certain direction, stand beside him, loving him, and he'll go down his own healing path at his own speed.

Don't try to get him to express anger; don't try to talk him out of sadness. Respond patiently and compassionately, no matter where he is on the healing journey.

I've been aware that some women think their men aren't moving fast enough. But consider the situation from his perspective. When I fought to overcome my painful background, I often chided myself for not moving faster. "I ought to be past these feelings," I said to myself several times.

One day as I said those words, a thought came to me. *You are where you need to be right now.* Was this the Spirit of God speaking? I don't know. But I do know that the simple statement gave me peace.

Try acknowledging to him and to yourself that he is, indeed, where he needs to be. It might take a long time for him to heal.

◆　◆　◆

Many years ago, a colleague talked to me about his troubled marriage. His wife had been sexually abused and would rarely allow sex. "Even when she agrees to have sex, she lies on the bed with about as much life as a rock." He complained for several minutes about her lack of response.

I wanted to help but I didn't know how. When he finished, I said, "I don't know what to tell you to do."

"Did I ask you for advice?" The anger in his voice shocked me. He wanted my sympathy, not my answers.

I apologized, and he talked for several more minutes. When he stopped, he thanked me for listening. "That helped a lot," he said.

When that significant person in your life begins to open up, he's not looking to you to give him answers. He's not looking to you for advice. He's looking to you for your support. It's easy to tell another what to do; it's difficult to listen and let him decide what to do. Too often people jump in with unasked-for advice.

Or they jump in when they're asked for advice. That's the tricky one.

If the man you care for asks, "What should I do?" Don't answer. Don't answer because that's not the real question. Even though it comes as a question, that doesn't mean he wants your advice. He might be saying he's confused. He might mean, "I can't trust my own judgment." You don't have to provide answers or push him to understand. That's his responsibility. Yours is to support him.

Once he's decided, support his choices—if you can. If you can't support a decision, explain your reason. My friend David treated me exactly right. He listened, and I could see the compassion on his face. He refused to advise me. He referred me to resources but nothing more than that. Although he is a psychologist, he put aside his role and functioned as my friend.

◆   ◆   ◆

Here's a statement that may surprise you. Too many people jump to God too quickly. When the man you love is in pain, and you know that you can't heal him, it's tempting right away to suggest that God can do the trick. God-talk is a sensitive area with many adult survivors. Some of us can't understand how a loving God could allow us to be molested. Some of us aren't ready to focus on God. Some of us were molested by those who claimed to be God's people.

Either allow him to bring up the topic or say something simple such as, "Would it be all right if we talked about God? I believe the Lord can help you." How do you know when it's okay to say even that? Be sensitive to his pain. If you can put away your own agenda and your sense of the best direction he should turn, and listen—truly listen—you're much more apt to know *when* to talk about how much Jesus Christ loves him and can help him.

One of my friends said, "Today I know that God is the answer to all the painful questions." He added that too many people want to blurt out the answer before they've fully heard the problem.

You don't want to be one of them.

✦   ✦   ✦

It's hard to stand by and watch someone you love struggle with pain. Many adult survivors were threatened or bribed by abusers to hold things inside. Holding the truth inside gets to be a difficult task, and that's one cause of the pain. But it's not easy to get beyond childhood fears and the threats to keep quiet.

It's just as difficult to change and to let the truth out. The survivor in your life didn't talk about his experience sooner for a variety of reasons. He may have been afraid to tell of his abuse because he didn't know whom to trust. He might have been fearful about how you would react. He might have thought you would blame him for the abuse. Maybe he'd been uncertain he could trust you.

Or he simply may not have been ready. If you want to help the man you care about, encourage him to tackle the past—at his own pace and in his own time. Gently remind him that he won't be able to move forward until he has healed the pains that began in his childhood and still linger.

Now, though, he needs your support. And this is where you'll need to exercise your strength to remain patient. He needs to know that you yearn for his healing, but he also needs to know that you'll accept the pace he sets and will walk beside him all the way.

REFUSE TO LET HIM JUSTIFY THE ABUSER

Years before I began to deal with my own abuse and I was still a pastor, Don visited my office. He told me about his incestuous relationship with his mother. It had begun with her fondling him as a child. After he reached puberty, he had sex with her regularly. "My dad just didn't have enough interest to satisfy her," he said.

His words shocked me. I had no idea how to talk to him. The relationship was clearly wrong, but whenever I tried to say something, he found a way to justify the incest. He was then thirty-two, and his mother was dying. He said that she asked him to have sex with her regularly until she died. "She needs me, so I said yes."

His case was probably the worst of justifying the abuser I've ever encountered. After listening for almost an hour and letting him push away my objections, I finally said, "Okay, Don. Tell me . . . why did you come here?"

He dropped his head into his hands. For what seemed several minutes he said nothing. "She loves me, but I don't . . . feel . . . right . . . about . . . about . . ."

"That's not love *for you*," I said. "That's putting her sexual needs above you." I tried to reason with him and explain not only that she had exploited him, but that she had sexually abused him.

He stared at me in shock. "She sexually abused me?" Still, even though he didn't feel right about doing it, he said he couldn't deny her dying wishes.

Don disappeared from my life after that. About ten years later he called me from Florida. He had gone through two divorces and had been in and out of mental institutions. "You were right about my mother," he said.

"I didn't need to be right," I said. "But I hope you've grown from the experience."

"I'm finally on the road to recovery." He had joined a Celebrate Recovery group. "I can talk about my problems and they listen."

His telling me I was correct wasn't much compensation. Although not as extreme as in Don's case, I'd many times heard victims justify their abusers. Because the perpetrator connived and skillfully convinced the victim that it wasn't wrong, the child obeyed but was left confused and often struggled to explain why it happened.

One of the things many recovering men have to cope with is self-blame. Sometimes the perpetrator put the idea into the head of the victim that he somehow caused his own abuse; sometimes the victim rationalized it. It's a way of saying, "I caused it."

A child doesn't cause sexual abuse. That's a reality the victim needs to learn. One way to help the man you care for accept that reality is not to allow him to justify or explain away the actions of the perpetrator.

Below are a few rationalizations he might make:

"I didn't stop it."

"I wanted/needed too much attention."

"He needed to feel loved."

"I was lonely."

"I came on to him."

"I was too affectionate and he didn't know where to stop."

"I dressed improperly."

"I was effeminate, and he probably thought I was gay."

Hear him out. Don't argue, but simply state, "You were a child. He abused you for his needs." Keep your statements simple. He may need to hear them many times.

The man who believes that his victimization is associated with being gay or effeminate may rationalize that this is the reason that the predator "came on to" him. Or a man might think that *because* he was abused by a male, he is now at risk of being gay or feminine. This man tends to become the macho-male. He often has trouble getting along in his work life and rarely can sympathize with others' feelings. He might constantly involve himself in activities that prove to the world and to himself that he is manly. He can't connect how he deals with the world today to his betrayal as a boy. He can't cry and face his suffering. He might even deny his childhood victimization and fight off feeling pain and shame.

However the man you care for justifies his abuser, arguing with him from logic is useless. In the beginning, the horror of the experience might find him telling you what happened and immediately justifying the assault: "He was a lonely man and unloved," he might say. "She needed me because I was the only one who cared about her."

Lovingly, tell him, "That was abuse. That wasn't caring for you."

Simply state the reality. Your role isn't to convince him; it is to stand by him as he faces the truth.

— *43* —

ENCOURAGE HIM TO BREAK THE SILENCE

We adult survivors often speak of the conspiracy of silence. Even when other members of the family suspect abuse, they maintain an aura of silence.

For me, breaking the silence was one of the most difficult areas of recovery. I didn't know how the others within the family would respond. For almost two weeks I tried to figure out how to go about it. Should I visit my hometown where my two brothers and three sisters still lived? Should I write a letter to each of them?

On Valentine's Day, one sister called me. We had a long discussion about a different subject. As we talked, calmness came over me and, without any mental preparation, I told her about the old man who had abused me.

To my relief and surprise, she added details about Mr. Lee that I had forgotten. At one point, I could hardly talk. *I've shattered the silence*, I kept thinking. *I've broken through.*

After that, she and I had several telephone conversations. Those calls helped me immensely. He had abused her but she hadn't known that he had also abused me.

A few months later, I visited my hometown. I spoke with a second sister. She had no idea of the first abuse by the woman who was a relative. I told her as much as I could remember. When I finished, she said, "I'm not surprised."

Her words shocked me. "What do you mean?"

She told me the female relative's mother had died when the woman was about eight years old. For the next two or three years, until her father remarried, he made her his sexual partner. That revelation didn't exonerate the woman, but it did give me more compassion for her.

I was glad I'd finally broken down the wall of silence. Once we siblings began to talk about such things, there was no longer strain or embarrassment. My sisters' confirmation that the abuse really happened was a great help to me. And beyond that, they helped me know that it was all right to talk about the pain. Later I talked to my brothers. After that, there was nothing hidden and it was freeing for me.

To shatter the silence can be a powerful step in recovery, but it has to be at the right time for the victim. One of the most significant factors in a victim's healing is for him to talk, especially to members of his family of origin. That might not always be practical, but it can be a powerful experience.

When he brings it up or when he's ready, encourage him. Depending on the circumstances, though, he might not get the positive, affirming results that I did. For example, a friend named Roy told his mother that his much older brother had abused him. "You always had such an active imagination," she said. That was the end of the discussion.

Her defensive response set him back and slowed his recovery.

Don't hold him back when he's ready. You may, though, need to help him accept the rejection or indifference of others. Regardless of the reactions of others, once he's broken the silence, he has taken long steps down the road of recovery. And you will be at his side.

44

ASK HIM TO CONSIDER PROFESSIONAL HELP

Lack of trust is an issue with men who were abused as children. It may prevent the man in your life from being open to professional counseling. For him to consider professional help might be difficult. Words such as psychiatrist, psychologist, counselor, or even therapy may cause him to hesitate. He may have heard bad stories (and they exist) or he may feel that his needing a professional would prove he's seriously ill. I suggest that the best thing for you to say is, "They help people with problems like yours. That's what they've been trained to do."

For some men, though, professional help isn't an option. It wasn't for me—at least not in the first years after my memories returned. As I mention earlier in this book, about three years into my healing-recovery, I joined a group of fifteen men under the guidance of two licensed counselors. By then, I was open enough to do so.

Aside from professional therapists, however, are the mutual-help groups. I've already mentioned Celebrate Recovery, which I heartily recommend. Another outstanding mutual-help group is Christians in Recovery, which has been in existence since 1992. See http://christians-in-recovery.org.

✦   ✦   ✦

Someone said, "Get support from your family; get therapy from your therapist." The spouses of victims can be extremely supportive.

They're close to us and they can understand our pain and offer us love and encouragement. Too many adult survivors, though, try to use their wives, mothers, or girlfriends as therapists.

Here's my advice to you as the significant woman in his life: don't take on that job—no matter how much it tempts you. The pain he must go through can place too great a strain on your relationship. Most people who are in any way involved in the healing of an adult survivor say it's unfair—and in some instances impossible—to expect the woman in his life to offer objective guidance or advice. If he seeks professional help, you best serve his therapy by being available after he has sessions. It's important for him to talk to you or to others who love and support him.

Shirley didn't become my therapist, but she was my reality check. After I made self-discoveries, I shared them with her. I didn't expect her to heal me, but I did want her to listen and to understand, and I moved forward. I made a statement to her that I believed in then and believe in even more today: "When I get beyond this, I will be different. If you don't stay connected to me, we'll still be married, but you won't know who I am."

She simply said, "I'm with you."

For her to say those few words was all I needed. I did the work. I read everything I could find. I talked to others who'd been abused. As I moved forward, I shared my experience with her and received many warm embraces from her.

In chapter 12 I talked about the mask that many adult survivors wear. Some men wear a smile even when talking about the most horrific of their experiences. Other men wear an expression of indifference even when they witness the sufferings of a loved one. Other men leer at women to hide their own insecurities about their masculinity. Removing that mask is one step in the healing process that could greatly benefit from professional help.

That's not to say you have no role in his unmasking. You *can* help the man in your life look carefully at himself and examine the motive for wearing the mask. When his words hurt or his behavior saddens you, you can remind yourself that they're a disguise and not who he truly is.

If you bring warmth and acceptance into the relationship, compassion and encouragement, you can help him peel off that perpetual smile or the frozen snarl. You can commend him for seeking the therapy that lets you see what's behind the cover-up—a wonderful, worthwhile person.

45

THE HEALING INFLUENCE OF WOMEN

Several women volunteered to share how they encouraged and challenged the abused men in their lives. Some have asked me to tell their stories for them, others tell their stories themselves.

Amy Cutler's Story

Amy Cutler's husband, Curtis, had been given up by his birth mother for adoption immediately after he was born. At age seven, he was adopted by the Dennings. "The first time I met my new dad," Curtis said, "he sexually abused me."

The new father, Daniel Denning, said to the boy, "No one has ever loved you." After he molested the boy he said, "This is what love is." The abuse lasted three years.

Although Amy and Curtis had met when she was ten and he was thirteen, a decade passed before they married. Before the wedding, Curtis told her he had been abused.

Denning abused many little boys, and Curtis thinks it might be as many as fifty. Denning was convicted twice of molestation. In 1996, the third time, Curtis was subpoenaed to testify at the trial. Denning was convicted and is in prison today.

After the trial, Curtis went into acute depression and was diagnosed with post-traumatic stress. In 1999, he attempted suicide by an overdose of prescription medication.

Amy and her daughters found Curtis and saved his life. He tried to push his family out of his life saying, "You need a man who can love you."

She and the daughters insisted, "You are the man we want."

Curtis went to counseling and so did Amy. Today they have a large support group at church. Both have found healing.

When I asked Amy how she helped her husband, she said, "One day God spoke distinctly to me: 'Get your hands off and keep your mouth shut. It's not your job and you don't know how to heal him.' Those words may sound harsh, but I needed to hear them because I wanted to heal my husband." She smiled and said, "So I held on and let God heal him."

Amy realized that she was to love and support him as his wife. She said, "I wasn't to be his parent to make him into a man. Mostly, I hung in with him. And God has brought healing to my husband and to our family."

Agatha's Story

Agatha attended a university in the Northwest and Dean worked in the same city. They met at the university, began to date, and Dean went to her church with her. That first Sunday, Dean spotted Ron, the man who had abused him.

Dean freaked out. He was so enraged, he said, "I'd like to kill the guy."

Dean had already begun to see a counselor named Scotty. After Dean explained what happened, Scotty followed up on the perpetrator and brought the two men together. Ron apologized and Dean forgave him.

A few weeks later, there was a party at Agatha's dorm and Dean came as a guest. The perpetrator also attended the party. He saw Dean and said hello.

"Outside. Now!" Dean said and led the way out of the dorm.

Agatha followed them.

Once they were outside, Dean said to Ron, "I forgave you, but we're not friends! Stay away from me. If you see me at an event like this, you leave. If you see her at any event"—he pointed at Agatha—"you leave."

Ron said nothing and left.

Agatha didn't understand the harsh boundaries, but she cared about Dean's recovery and supported him. She has stood by Dean as he's taken each step in his healing and growth and will continue to do so. She admits that sometimes she doesn't understand his decisions but she believes he's doing the best for himself that he knows how.

She assumes it's because his boundaries were violated as a child that he has set up rigid ones for his own protection. Even now he'll sometimes say things quite adamantly such as, "Boys do not babysit." "Our children cannot have sleepovers." "We do not leave our kids in the child-care of James" (a neighbor).

Agatha's husband has suffered, and although she doesn't understand his reasoning and occasionally his decisions make life awkward or inconvenient, she loves him and supports his decisions.

She says, "Dean hasn't talked publicly about his abuse. I told him that I would wait for him to tell his story when he's ready. That's the reason I've chosen to remain anonymous."

Mary Tells Her Story

The abused man in my life was Arnie, my oldest son. We adopted Arnie when he was seven years old and didn't know that he'd been sexually abused. I was so innocent at that time, I didn't know those kinds of things happened to children. I was completely unprepared for what that abuse did to our lives.

When he was a child, he sought predators to continue to abuse him, even after he moved into our safe home. The sexual abuse dominated our lives for years.

It may help to tell you a little of his background. His primary abuser was his stepgrandfather, for whom he had been named. His biological mother was a prostitute, and Arnie was also abused by several men she brought into their home. By the time he was twelve years old, he regularly met men in public restrooms to engage in sexual activity.

Once I learned about his activities, I did everything I could to protect him from further abuse. No matter what I did, however, he seemed to be a magnet for more abuse.

Arnie, in turn, abused others and hurt anyone who was innocent enough to trust him. I thus spent much of my energy trying to protect the innocent from him.

We put him in counseling through our church and child services but the professional counselors avoided the subject completely. I realize now that they had no idea how to help him, so they focused on other areas where they could help. They also talked to my husband and me, and we discussed mundane things such as his school performance, his relationships, and our parenting. No matter how often or how long we talked, the counselors always avoided the so-called "elephant in the room."

Arnie was a sweet-but-tormented boy. He had no understanding about what drove him into sexual activity. Many times he collapsed into my arms in tears, crying, "Why do I do these things?"

Arnie believed he had "tainted genes." I don't believe it had anything to do with tainted genes and that it had everything to do with generational sin. I'm sure that his grandfather had been abused by the men in his life.

I realized that my role in Arnie's life was to love him and do what I could to protect the world from his terrible drives.

Arnie died of AIDS in 1997 at the age of twenty-nine. The last year of his life, he returned to God and we had a good year together. We got a glimpse of what a healthy and whole Arnie would be like.

I originally gave you permission to use my name but my younger son asked me to withdraw it because "it will make people wonder about me and if anything happened to me."

Zeta Gibb Tells Her Story

Although he was six foot three, wiry and strong, with oversized hands, my brother-in-law, Art, seemed fragile to me. Despite his ability to talk with anyone, anywhere, about anything, I sensed he was like an insecure little boy, even though my view contradicted the face of the evidence. I learned to keep my opinions to myself.

When Art was in a room, no one else had to speak. If those around him would let him, he'd fill every nanosecond. One contradictory memory sticks out.

One evening he was grilling meat. During a twenty-minute period, I counted exactly fifty times he asked for reassurance that he grilled properly. As I watched my sister, I wondered how she kept her sanity married to a man who was so needy. As it turned out, she didn't.

Both my sister's mental stability and their marriage disintegrated. After their breakup, Art lived with my husband and me. It wasn't easy but we believed it was the right thing for us to do.

Art continually repeated how much he loved his wife and daughter, but his voice lacked the feeling behind the words. Although Art pushed people to a safe distance, I was able to slip in beneath his defenses.

Knowing the danger of crossing the line between counselor and family, I treaded carefully with Art. I helped him learn to recognize when he was running away in fear and when he wasn't honest with himself or me. He tired of my saying, "You're holding your breath. What are you afraid of?"

I tried to talk with Art about Jesus and his love. If God entered the conversation, Art changed the subject. He had a particularly impatient streak for anything to do with the concept of a heavenly Father. My husband and I prayed that the seeds would someday grow.

Art and I worked through the difference between loving and possessing. He came to see that he kept people at a distance. Revelations and insight came and went, because nothing stayed learned. Everything in my professional training screamed major trauma.

Late one night, he finally gave me the clue I needed. Art had no memories of his twelfth year of life. He and his mother had moved to a different city after his eleventh birthday. They returned soon after he turned twelve. I suggested he needed professional help to unearth what had happened in that lost year.

After a few more weeks of late night talks, Art came to a decision I'd been praying he'd make. "Talking with you hurts too much. It's too painful. I can't leave. I have nowhere else to go, but I need help. My life's a mess. I've decided to see a shrink."

He did just that. During his sessions the secrets of his past surfaced. I knew the psychiatrist was making progress by the degree of anger Art expressed. The more he referred to my sister as useless and stupid, the more I sensed Art was getting at his true feelings.

Then Art avoided us. He spent days locked in his room. On occasions, he joined us for a meal and ate in sullen silence.

One day, the dam of his memories burst in a horrific flood. When I came home, Art was sitting in the family room shaking. Gasping and choking, he told me what had happened during the blank year. Every month, instead of paying rent, his mother "turned him over" to the landlord and his friends. He didn't graphically describe what he endured, but his body language spoke for him. We cried while I rocked him in my arms.

Things my sister complained about began to make sense. Art's enormous demands for sex to prove he wasn't homosexual from the experience had turned that area of their life into a nightmare. He blamed her for business reversals or lost opportunities. He treated his daughter as an ornament, a product of his masculinity.

Another evening, after I returned home from work, Art again sat in the family room trembling. When I asked what had happened, he said, "I almost didn't get to come home today."

"What do you mean?"

"They thought they'd have to commit me. I started reliving the experiences and my therapist said she couldn't get me to come back. I snapped out of it just as she was calling to have them come get me. I was seeing and feeling the abuse again. He came at me and made me—"

He stopped abruptly, unable to talk about the memories.

I took his hand. "You don't have to tell me."

He nodded and said nothing. I stayed with him until he became calm.

Art healed enough to moderate his treatment of women, but still refused my attempts to talk about God. Later, he remarried and bought a home with his new wife.

Art's life changed when he was diagnosed with pancreatic cancer. The anger returned, disguised as meanness and unreasonable demands. All that was left for the rest of us to do was to care for his failing body and pray to rescue his drowning soul.

When the end was near, his wife, Sue, called hospice to get him. Art rocked back and forth and cried out, "Hold me. I need help. Hold me. Bless my head. Bless my mouth. Bless, bless . . . I need help, hurry. Hold me. Bless, uh, bless . . ."

Sue held her husband. Minutes later, the hospice staff prepared to take him away. Sue left the room to sign papers.

I knelt beside Art and said. "Heaven is real and Jesus is real."

Art balled up his right fist and with his arm bent at the elbow brought his fist up chest high before driving it sharply toward the bed. "I *know* it!"

Barely able to contain my excitement, I said, "Jesus loves you."

Cradled in my arms like a rag doll, he said, "I know."

The feelings expressed in his tone of voice told me this was precious to him. He clearly believed. I gently caressed Art's head and said, "You know Jesus has you."

"Okay." He straightened and said again, "*Okay!*" Immediately he became calm.

Fourteen hours later, he died, never having uttered another word.

Sharon Roe's Story

In an earlier chapter, Gary Roe wrote about the way we met at a conference. Sharon, his wife, writes her perspective:

The big thing I've learned through Gary's experience is that darkness hates light. When darkness is exposed, it loses its power. Opening myself and our family to the pain caused by what happened to Gary has been the hardest thing I've ever done. Just as a dirty wound will fester, so the abuse heaped on Gary would cause more anguish and pain if left untended. Believing that kept me going. I knew the real Gary was buried under the weight of the burden he carried. He tried to be perfect in every situation yet he always seemed haunted, blaming himself for being less than perfect no matter how remarkable the results.

I had no idea what lay ahead. Many days I wanted to slam the front door and drive as far away as I could get. Many nights I awoke, hearing Gary pace the floor through another sleepless night, unable to let down his guard for a moment. Or worse, I awakened to his sobs as memories stole his sleep from him.

Yet those days and nights were the fuel for my resolve to stay with him. If he couldn't let down his guard and sleep with me lying beside him, how could he be open with me during the waking hours? In spite of twenty-three years of marriage, I realized I had felt alone throughout most of them. Our periods of intimacy were mostly confined to vacations, when Gary could relax enough to push away everything else. And I wanted to see more of that healthy side of Gary.

I encouraged Gary to take the time he needed to heal. We both saw counselors, and he shared the truth not only with our family, but with our congregation as well. Those positive steps carried us through, yet not without difficulty. But it would have been helpful [for him] to have others to talk to about how it felt—others who had been through it and come out the other side.

The day Gary met Cec was a turning point. He had finally talked with someone who could understand! It was wonderful to see Gary open up. He wasn't so alone, and he felt less branded by shame. I had done what I could, but Gary couldn't totally accept my viewpoint because I was not in the fraternity. Having another man to talk to lessened Gary's fear and his feelings of powerlessness. Cec was another *man* who had survived and was no less a man. My part has been to reassure Gary that it was both okay to open the wound and that I would stick by him and love him. I have fought alongside him against the mind-bending accusations the abuse taught him to accept as true.

Ever so slowly, the wounds are being cleansed, and he lives with more freedom. Our relationship is moving toward an openness I never dreamed possible. We have chosen the light.

HE NEEDS YOU

In summary, here are a few suggestions so you can help the man you care for move more quickly through his recovery.

Be honest about your feelings. Don't lie or try to hide how you feel.

Try to be a reflective listener. That is, pay attention and give consideration to his thoughts and feelings.

Seek eye contact. Look at him as he talks.

Do whatever you can to make him feel safe with you.

Suggest regular times to talk. Everything he needs to say won't all come out in one conversation. He might not know what he wants to say, or he may be unwilling to divulge more. As he speaks and you accept his words, it enables him to probe deeper into his past. As he probes, he heals.

Accept him as he is. He won't be perfect at the end of his healing journey. Accept his idiosyncrasies or quirks.

Recognize that healing won't always be in one straight line. After months of progress and increasing intimacy, he may suddenly reject you or create distance. Be patient. Think of it as a time-out for him.

Realize that you may project your attitude or values on him. Be careful. Your own childhood experiences may affect your attitude.

When appropriate, remind him that you love him, that you pray for him, and that God has always loved him.

Keep your expectations for him realistic. Avoid keeping a mental calendar of when he should be healed or how quickly he should be able to move forward.

Accept the pace of his progress, even if it's not as fast as you'd like. This is *his* painful past, not yours.

Forego the temptation to say what *you think* he wants to hear. Speak the truth. If the truth might hurt, don't say it when he's still vulnerable.

Avoid blaming him for the problems in your relationship. He has probably done many things wrong. Accept that it was the best way he knew to cope.

Live in the present, and encourage him to do so as well. He needs to empty himself of the trauma of his childhood, but that doesn't have to control his thoughts so much that he holds on to resentments and anger of the past.

Accept that you may not know what's best for him. You may, but what if you don't?

＋　＋　＋

Sexual abuse is one of the worst torments a boy can go through. It attacks his physical, spiritual, and psychological integrity. If you are committed to help the adult survivor in your life, you can be a true heroine in his life.

He needs someone.

He needs you.

I hurt for a long time because of childhood sexual abuse, and I wanted to provide a safe place where hurting men could connect with other survivors of sexual abuse. Visit www.menshatteringthesilence.blogspot.com.